CASEY

James & Elle

James & Elle

ISBN: 978-1-923163-07-2 (Paperback)

A catalogue record for this work is available from the National Library of Australia

Cover Design: Lauren Woodall https://www.kissthesky.com.au
Format and Typeset: Clark & Mackay
Self-Published by Casey Rae with assistance by Clark & Mackay

Proudly printed in Australia by Clark & Mackay

Contents

Author's note

Firstly, thank you for picking up this book. It has been many years in the making and I am so grateful for its beautiful embodiment. In crafting this autofiction novel, it was important to me to explore personal experiences, memories, and emotions in a raw and authentic manner. While the events and characters portrayed within these pages are inspired by real-life encounters, it is essential to note that names and places have been altered to safeguard the privacy of those involved.

By changing names and locations, I have created a safe space for both the individuals who inspired these stories and the readers who engage with them. This decision allows for a more open and honest exploration of the themes and emotions at the heart of this work while respecting the privacy and confidentiality of those who have played a part in James and Elle's journey. The author's recollection of other characters and implied criminal acts may or may not, in the future, face punishment in the eyes of the law. However, the revelations that lie in the pages of this novel—read by you—will be justice enough.

It is my hope that, through this autofiction narrative, readers will find resonance and connection, recognising the universal aspects of human experience that transcend specific individuals and settings. By protecting privacy and delving deeper into the essence of these stories, the narrative focuses on the emotions and ideas they evoke rather than the identities of those involved.

Thank you for embarking on this literary journey with me, and I hope that the altered names and places within this autofiction novel will allow you to fully immerse yourself in the narrative while respecting the privacy of all individuals involved.

I acknowledge the Worimi and Biripi people as the traditional custodians of the land and waterways from which I live and write. It always was, and always will be, Aboriginal land. I celebrate the songlines, stories, culture, and traditions of Aboriginal and Torres Strait Islander Elders of all communities.

A special shout out to all my supporters. I love you deeply. Denise, Joel, Tyler, Kate, Maria, Fern, Ashari, Jessica, Megan, Kerrie, Sammy and Robyn—thank you for continually holding space for me.

CHAPTER 1

Elle—Apathy—2021

Elle absently watches the name *James* flash across her screen as the phone rattles and jumps along the kitchen bench, screeching and demanding. She inhales deeply through her pursed lips and turns the phone over facedown with one hand while the other continues stirring the pot of bolognese bubbling on the stove. Elle tries to ignore the image her mind conjures of her brother pressing the red button on his Samsung, swearing out loud when she doesn't answer, James's lanky body hunching over a coffee table laden with an overflowing ashtray, a broken ice pipe, lighters, and crinkled porn magazines, overgrown fingernails hastily rolling a cigarette, his dark algae eyes darting around a dull room filled with smoke, reeking of spilt rum, spit, and dirty socks. Elle watches him from the shadows of her imagination; he is twitching, his knee bouncing frantically. In her cabinet of memories, she hears James call her name.

She shrugs away the illusion, shudders, and spies the split second Asher reaches up to the bowl of grated cheese, catching the lip with his grubby fingers. The bowl somersaults to the kitchen floor, a confetti of cheese scattered around their feet.

"Asher!" Elle scolds, her tone more aggressive than she intended. Her brother's imposition on her quiet home life rattles her more these days than ever before.

Asher is blissfully ignorant of his mum's tone. His eighteen months of life have yet to teach him about other people's emotions, and he happily scoops up strands of cheese, his blonde head bobbing between Elle's shins and the cupboard drawer. Elle makes a mental note that she needs to wipe down the cupboards after dinner tonight and then acknowledges how she would rather watch Netflix and instead convinces herself that she will clean the cupboards at least before the weekend. Definitely before Sunday night when Mum arrives.

* * *

It's dark in the cupboard and Ellie has her delicate hands folded over her body. Her breath is loud and quick. She is tucked between some clothes hanging from the bar above her head. She can see light filtering in between the slats in the old timber frame. With her knees pressed up against her chin, she can hear his voice outside. Loud laughter. A cuss word she knows she must not use. A question she does not answer. The silhouette looms closer. Elle's small frame sinks deeper between the clothes, even though he knows she is in there. This is a game they play. Ellie does not like this game. She feels nervous and vulnerable but is too young to know these words yet. This is a game her brother plays when her mum goes out. Elle wishes he would let her leave her clothes on when he tells her to get into the closet.

* * *

Elle awakes to the flashing light of her phone insisting she open her eyes and reads the message from Lily, James's girlfriend.

Sorry to contact you so late at night, but I finally heard from James. Call me when you wake up.

Elle looks at the time: 4:27 am. It's the middle of winter and the fire has gone out. Her arms bristle against the cold. Elle sighs and heaves the doona over her body, wrestling her head into her pillow. She breathes in heavily, wondering if she can hear Asher snoring from the room next door. Satisfied he isn't waking, Elle allows her mind to wander. She wonders what Lily will tell her—is her brother alive and well? Is he cooped up in a drug den in Washington? Is he cold and wet on the Appalachian trail? Where is he?

There is no more sleep. Elle reluctantly—and a little resentfully—drags herself from bed at 5:15 am when she hears Asher calling from his cot—"Maamaa, Maamaa-aa"—and together they commence the morning routine. Boob, nappy, grown-up toilet, prep for breakfast.

At 6:37 am, Elle's phone vibrates across the dining table. It's Lily. Could she not wait for Elle to make the call? It must be important. But isn't it always? Elle sighs and sips her hot broth, pushing toast closer to Asher's disinterested clapping hands.

Elle remembers when she first met Lily, at Christmas a couple of years ago. Of course, James had been raving about this "angel" and "soul mate" with a clover tattoo, sent to guide him through these "dark, dark days." James talked about Lily as though she knew all about his deepest demons and the precise way to soothe his nightmares, and she still loved him unconditionally. Elle imagined Lily to be strong-headed and steadfast in her convictions—religious, maybe. But Elle wasn't quite prepared for the whimsical, twenty-something waif who glided through her front door on that hot and stuffy Christmas Eve wearing a crocheted bra and a long cheesecloth skirt. Lily's thin blonde hair fell limply around her shoulders, collarbone catching the stringy strands. Elle's impulse was to scream at Lily to stop loving her brother, to tell her to run, run far away. But instead, Elle met Lily with a warm embrace, pulling her close and smelling coconut, lavender, and tobacco smoke.

Asher is still clapping his hands when Elle finally taps the green icon on the phone screen to answer Lily's call. *Shhh*, she mimes. *Clap, clap, clap*, flaps Asher.

"Hi, Lily." Elle forces a smile as though this is a regular tell-me-how-amazing-your-holiday-has-been kind of call.

"Hey, Elle." Lily doesn't force a thing. Naturally effortless. Lily takes a deep breath. Her words are slow and calculated, rehearsed, but nerves—or worry—hinder the delivery.

"So, I woke up to a message from James. He … He … I don't think he is well. In the message he was, like, saying he had no shoes, no phone, no meds, no cards, and um, he was yelling at people." Lily's thin voice tapers at the end.

"Okay. What was he saying?" Elle sips her bone broth, licks her lips, and crosses her legs.

"Um, he was ranting. You know. Saying he would kill someone."

"Oh." Elle stands up, lifts Asher out of his highchair, and puts him onto the floor, where he runs free into the living room, a trail of crumbs falling in his wake.

Lily continues, "I'm not sure, but I think he needs help. Like a doctor. Or hospital. Or something."

"Hmm. Yeah, sounds like it." Elle looks at the clock on the wall and listens to the *tick tick*. Asher's *vroom vroom* in the room next door. The chickens' *cluck cluck* outside.

Eventually, Lily speaks again. "Anyway, I just wanted to let you know …"

Elle hears Lily shuffling, moving and twisting her body in that grotesquely beautiful way.

"Yeah. Thanks, Lily. I guess I can call the consulate, maybe the DVA, see what I can do. But right now, I need to get Asher dressed and off to day care."

"Aw, yeah, totally. Okay. Um, yeah, so just let me know how

you go." Lily's tone is the most energetic it has been during the whole conversation. Elle feels a slight pang of remorse.

"Well, try not to worry," she offers. "But thanks for letting me know. I'll see what I can do."

"Okay. Thanks, Ez. Hey—" Lily starts, then pauses. Elle scoops Asher up into her arms and smiles at him. He pushes his face into hers and lets a loud "wooooow" escape his little cherry-pip mouth.

"You know, I really do love him. I just want him home. After everything that has happened, I just need him back here in Australia." Lily sniffs into the phone.

Elle's lips purse and her eyes glance up at the ceiling, but she responds with as much compassion as she can muster. "Yeah. Me, too, Lil. Me, too."

Somewhere, buried beneath years of burden, stress and thankless support, Elle nearly means what she says.

* * *

Later that day, Elle is watching Asher play in the sandpit. He has found a pool of water in the old sink that was placed under the frangipani tree earlier in the season by his dad, Bryce. Asher's khaki pants are soaked up to his knees, evidence of how he climbed into the sink and sat for a confused moment, baffled by the encroaching coolness up his legs. Asher rolls out of the sink and back into the sand, looking like a crumbed calamari tentacle wriggling on the sand. Asher squeals with excitement as he throws a cardboard toilet paper roll into the sink and watches it darken and then disappear under water. *Where did he get that from?* Elle muses over its origin.

As she sits on the verandah in a rickety and slightly mouldy wooden garden chair, Elle looks across at the garden of salad greens and grape vines. Her appreciation for Bryce surges in a wave that she rarely feels these days. Her husband is a hard worker and has invested endless after-hours into generating the once grass-only garden to become a sustainable and kid-friendly space. The sand pit, the climbing frame around the frangipani tree, the sandstone path that curls around the pawpaw trunk, the pond with terrified tadpoles and a collection of trucks and spoons sunk to the bottom. Asher loves accumulating insects and he has not yet learnt to stop picking the tadpoles out of their watery oasis. Elle is often pinching the wriggling amphibians and plopping them back into the bucket. Bryce's passion for permaculture had inspired and motivated Elle to research, cook, and explore food in a way she hadn't before. Elle has fed from his knowledge, learning how to preserve, ferment, and dehydrate herbs, fruits and vegetables. Bryce works tirelessly on growing food while Elle works tirelessly in the kitchen. As an adult, Elle had achieved the simple life she always wanted, far from the chaos and drama of her childhood, adolescence, and twenties. Now, nearing forty, Elle has finally found pockets of calmness.

Until, of course, James needed her.

CHAPTER 2

James—Hiking—2021

It's pretty wild to be abroad again, James thinks as he plants one foot in front of the other. It's been a while since he's passed anyone on the trail. Rhythmically, he lurches along the twisting path, where wispy strands of bushy bluestem snatch at his cargo pants. James's pack is heavy and his shoulders are sore, but not as sore as his calf muscles. Red-hot jolts sear up his leg as he climbs the sloping mountain. This is his fourth day on the Appalachian Trail, and James is already noticing the blisters forming on his ankles and his left little toe. The Great Smoky Mountains National Park in Tennessee has proven to have its challenges. After all the training James completed back in Australia to achieve peak physical shape—all the weight-lifting, cross-fit, and hours of research on YouTube—James did not expect the hike to be this taxing on his body. He believed, after all he had endured in his thirty-something years of living, that a walk in the woods would be simple. It was the simplicity he was craving.

As darkness begins to suffocate the sunlight, James sets up camp on the edge of a mossy collection of tall eastern white pine trees, standing postcard-proud. He avoids the designated camping spots, as he is not keen on making small talk with the other hikers. James rolls out the self-inflating sleeping mat, warms some noodles using the gas cooker, and guzzles the water he has left in his canister.

Somewhere a coyote howls. Birds cry as they soar across the inky sky, taking refuge in the tall pines. James stares up at the mottled sky, feeling the expanse stretching on and on and on. He thinks of all the steps he still needs to take on this mammoth trail. One foot in front of the other. Step. Step. Step.

Two months, three weeks, and two days to go. James desperately needs this experience to heal his broken mind, release his trauma, and shake him free of the memories. Until now, nothing else has worked.

Tonight's mountain air is deathly still—thick with the sounds of summer insects yet without a breath of a breeze. James slouches in solitude, his thoughts drifting as he fusses about the exposed campsite. After he has eaten, he takes out a large plastic ziplock bag from a hidden compartment of his backpack. Rolling the plastic bag between his fingers, James sighs with contentment. Before James left Australia, his psychiatrist, Dr Wilson, signed off on the paperwork for the Department of Veterans Affairs to assure James's rehabilitation case worker that walking the Appalachian Trail would be the best treatment for his PTSD. James was grateful for Dr Wilson—she always seemed to be in his corner. She answered his calls after hours. She called him when he missed appointments—which was frequently. She wrote him many referrals to clinics, specialists, and experts. Plus she gave him the right medication. Knowing that James would be in remote parts of the Virginia and Tennessee wilderness, she agreed to give James three months' supply of his medication that he could take on his walking therapy: Seconal for sleeping, clonazepam for anxiety, Prozac for depression, and a couple of other essentials James would need along the way. With a bundle of green paper prescriptions legally signed, James had to visit six different chemists to have them all filled. There were limits on how many meds of this potency were allowed to be dispensed at one time, which James knew was one way "the system" tried to support people struggling with their mental health who may want to top themselves. James understood the sentiment. After he had cleverly collected three months' supply, he popped the tablets from the foil and combined them into a ziplock bag that he stuffed into a console of his hiking rucksack.

Three months' supply, thanks to Dr Wilson's trusting and professional nature.

In just four days, James had already taken two weeks' worth of medication. And tonight, under the dusky sky, he will take another handful of colourful pills.

* * *

Thirty hours later, James finds himself outside of Washington Station. He tries to remember the sequence of events, but his memory is blurry. He had lit the fire and had definitely eaten something—whatever it was now made him feel nauseous—and he remembers seeing a group of people hiking towards him and their casual conversation. One man asked whether they could camp with him; James groggily agreed. One of the blokes offered James a beer and while he should have said "no thanks", the concoction of pills was starting to make James woozy and incoherent. The foreign people in his personal space made him feel anxious. Remembering how easy it was to communicate with strangers after a few beers and sincerely lacking clarity, he agreed to a drink, which turned into three beers and then, suddenly, someone was opening a bottle of whiskey.

James grabs at his throbbing head, pulsing like the train behind him pulling into the station. People are staring. People are taking photos as they walk past. James spins on the spot and stumbles, hands hitting the concrete. He sees his feet, purple knobbly toes and festering blisters on his ankles. Where are his hiking boots?

James lurches upright, screams at someone walking by, "Where are my fucking shoes?" But the person keeps walking, quickly, in the other direction. The loudness and the chaos of the station make James dizzy. He needs to find his backpack, his meds, his phone. James is snatching at his clothes, realising he isn't wearing a shirt. He finds his phone in a pocket of his grubby cargo pants. He checks the battery and feels a slight pang of relief. Two bars.

He has enough brainpower to consider his options. He could call his sister, Elle, but she is likely to hang up on him, and he can't risk losing the last of his battery. Fumbling with the screen, he calls Lily. She will know what to do.

CHAPTER 3

Divorce—1991

When James was three, Elle seven, and Lance nearly twelve, Pearl left her husband, Simon—or did he leave her? That's the problem with time: memories become debatable. In the future, the memories from each side of the embittered and failed marriage become blurred with resentment, unrequited love, and the overarching lack of emotional support.

On the day of separation, Pearl suggests they stay together as a family for the children. Simon replies, "You expect me to look after your children while you go out?"

Pearl angrily reminds him, "They are your children, too! I didn't make them by myself, although I have been raising them alone for ten years!" Next, something is thrown and someone swears—neither will admit it was them.

And so, Simon moves to Sydney, continuing to earn a decent income and build a career for himself, and he kindly makes time every second weekend to see the children. Friends and strangers comment, *It's so great to see a dad spending time with his children.*

Simon won't talk to Pearl again, carrying his resentment and unrequited love well into his seventies, because Simon's memories of the events leading up to the divorce are slightly different. He remembers working really hard to provide for his family, leaving home early and arriving home late, all so that the children could play sports and have nice things to wear and a home to live in that overlooks the water. Simon remembers being incredibly overworked and that, on the weekends, he just needed—deserved—a sleep-in. His job was busy and he spent long days making presentations and delivering pitches to prospective clients. Therefore, when he arrived home, he needed some peace and quiet to recharge. Pearl would hush the children so he could read his book at the dining table, and when the little whirlwinds would not stop yabbering at him and asking him to play, he bought himself some headphones. Simon could disappear downstairs, smoke his pipe, and listen to blues music cry to him through the speakers. Simon did not think there was a problem with this arrangement until Simon came home early one Tuesday afternoon after a work meeting had been cancelled and found Pearl in bed with another man.

Over the years, Simon's story of betrayal becomes more enraged, and Pearl's story of broken communication and loneliness softens and mellows. Time is powerful.

Nonetheless, Pearl soon meets another man who she thinks will be forever. Don.

Don is a striking man, tall, silver-haired, tanned, with wide blue eyes and a Crocodile Dundee style. He won't be in her life forever, merely a few tumultuous years. Don wins Pearl's heart with his outdoorsy lifestyle. He catches her fish and takes her to quiet beaches where they sleep in the dunes under the star-lit sky. Don is rugged and aloof, but jovial and kind. He loves Pearl and desires her with more lust than Simon ever did.

Simon had been a bookish, computer-using, administrative, suit-wearing, city-lovin' kind of man. He spent his time chasing a successful career, working 6 am to 7 pm and getting home just in time to briefly tickle the kids, give them a sweet treat, and say goodnight. The children all have varied recollections of the time their parents were married. James does not have any memories at all of when Simon lived with them at Koolewong. James's memories start at age five, when he went to Dad's apartment every second weekend and had his fill of sugar, arcade games, movies, and expensive and frivolous gifts. After the weekend, James would catch the train home on a Sunday with his big sister Elle, arms full of junk food and plush toys won at Timezone and, as they finally arrived at Koolewong station, Pearl would be waiting patiently for them to disembark. James acutely remembers the one time Pearl's boyfriend, Don, was waiting there instead. His large frame stood just past the yellow safety line, arms crossed.

This particular night, Don was looking after the kids while Pearl was out—playing tennis, maybe—and James was acting out a little. Six-year-old James was screaming after dinner and demanding ice cream. Don was having none of it.

"You didn't finish your dinner. No dessert!" Don screamed.

"Ahhhhhh! You're not my dad!" James countered as he raced down the hallway and slammed his bedroom door.

Elle watched the silhouettes stomp past her door, which was halfway down the hallway. Shortly after James's outburst, Don followed, bellowing, "Never slam the door in this house, you little punk!" and he pushed the door open, heaving with anger.

* * *

Elle is eleven and James is nearly seven years old. They are squashed into the back seat of a Land Rover, bumpily travelling at eighty kilometres an hour down a country highway, soft toys, empty water bottles, two odd socks, a pair of green gumboots, and a crumpled book crowding around them. Don, blue-eyed, with three-day stubble across his chin, is driving, and Pearl is sitting in the passenger seat, concentrating on a crossword puzzle.

Outside, little James can see the flat, red earth of western New South Wales—Wongaibon Country. In the distance, he thinks he can see two emus running towards a scattered tree line, but as he blinks, the birds disappear into spirals of dust.

"Oi! Catch!" Elle kicks James's foot and simultaneously throws two odd socks rolled into a little ball straight at her little brother's blonde head. James screeches in complaint and then gathers the socks and giggles.

He leans back against the window, hoists his lean legs up into an arc over the middle seat, and hurls the socks back at his sister. She ducks and they hit the window with a soft *thoooin*. James and Elle laugh quietly.

Elle collects the socks and starts a little chant. "Here come the socks. The socks, the socks, the socks. Here come the socks; better duck, or they will feel like rocks," and she throws them, hard, at James. He catches them. Laughter erupts again.

Pearl jerks around, and the kids cover their mouths with sticky hands. Elle catches Don's eyes in the rear-view mirror. Slowly, she reaches for the socks, tucks them in the side console of the door, and turns away from an expectant James to gloomily peer out the window. James huffs and puts his head in his hands.

They have been on the road for two weeks now, Don's '85 Land Rover towing a yellow and grey pop-top caravan he bought for six hundred dollars a few months ago. It didn't take him much to convince Pearl to tour New South Wales in an old caravan. At first, she was hesitant about James and Elle missing time from primary school, but eventually agreed when Don showed her photos of the wide open spaces where they would be camping. After years of living at Albany Street, consisting of parenting, housework, minding the neighbour's children, and only one holiday in six years, Pearl was craving some spontaneity and adventure, although she was concerned about leaving her eldest son, Lance. Since the divorce, he had become sombre and earnest. On a few occasions, Lance had left a note on his downstairs bedroom door—*I've gone to Dad's*—and would be gone for a few days. Each time, Pearl called Simon to make sure Lance had arrived safely, and Simon replied bluntly—"Yes, he's here"—without elaborating. Eventually, after a few nights away, he skulked his way back through the garage and into his room, lighting a cigarette. Pearl could smell it drifting up the stairwell. Pearl knew she had to speak with her teenage son. She knocked on his door and smiled sweetly, slowly sitting on the edge of his bed. But Lance was moody and did not say much at all; instead, he asked her to leave his room. As soon as the door was closed, music pulsated through the house like a heart attack.

When Pearl decided to leave Lance alone at home—aged nearly seventeen—she was concerned he would host a party and ruin the house while they were away, but Don was very persuasive. And so it was decided: after the holiday in the caravan, upon their return, Pearl and the younger kids would move to the farm that Don owns; Lance would stay in the two-storey home nestled in the national park until it was sold. Pearl was satisfied, although apprehensive, about this plan. Yet she figured that, if the kids and Don could get along while living in a caravan for a few weeks, they could cut ties with the house on Albany Street, and finally all of the memories with Simon, and then the next chapter of their lives would be a fresh start. And anyway, Lance would be nearly ready to move away for university. He was a young man now. Pearl convinced herself that this was the best solution for her family's happiness. Besides, she was very happy with Don.

Don had friends scattered across the countryside. Hunters and farmers and hillbillies with names like Birdie, Billy the Kid, Jacko, and Slim. Don had spent most of his forty years living off the land—fishing, camping, jackarooing his way from place to place. He knew places where they could camp for free, catch fish and rabbits, and sleep under the stars. Knowing this, Pearl was simply smitten. Her eyes lit up and her heart raced. This was the adventure she had been waiting for when she was with Simon, but it never came. Simon's expensive and fast lifestyle meant he was a slave to his job, paying off debt and working harder to buy more gadgets.

This particular morning, Pearl wakes at dawn, stretches, and climbs out of the caravan, careful not to wake her snowy-haired children. Don is already awake and has stoked the fire, the blackened billy on to boil. Pearl looks out across the campsite, past the grey gums and early morning fog gathered among the spindly fingers of the box grass. Between the fog and the marshmallow sky hovers a dusky mountain top, perched as though floating above the clouds. Pearl inhales the smell of damp air, campfire smoke, and drying eucalypts. She yawns. Deep inside her, her heart swells with contentment, and an unusual wave of stillness circles her. Pearl's life has been tumultuous and, at times, arduous. Her father was a violent man, and her early memories of him reminded her of a life she did not want for her own children. When Pearl's dad left for another woman, Pearl's mother was left with six kids scrambling underfoot and very little money to feed and clothe them. Pearl, being the eldest, mothered her siblings while her own mother turned to the bottle to escape the pain of her reality. At sixteen, Pearl had moved out of home and was working, sending cash back to her family when she could. Her siblings had been divided up between two households and there was a part of Pearl that regretted not being able to help them more. Now, in her late forties, Pearl loves her family with her whole being. Her body aches for them, to help, to serve, to be together. In the future, when Pearl finds out the truth about her own children, she will still cling to the longing for her family to be together no matter what. But for now, Pearl is blissfully unaware of the pain to follow and, instead, enjoys the moment of stillness and clarity in the remote Australian bush.

Her long-legged daughter slithers from the caravan and Pearl curls an arm around her.

"I need to pee," Ellie giggles, and the two pick their way past the remains of the campfire, around the towering swirl of gum trees, and slowly down an embankment towards a midnight-coloured dam.

"Stop!" Pearl squeezes Elle's arm.

Surrounding the mirrored water, a mob of kangaroos stare, picture frozen, ears pricked. Slowly, one by one, the roos decide the two figures are of no danger, and they begin to drink the murky water and nibble the sweet grass. Pearl and Ellie watch them for minutes, in silence, before the roos turn and thump their way through the trees and the fog.

Pearl and Elle turn to each other and smile, mother and daughter caught in a moment of peace and serenity. This precious memory is laced with peace—a peace neither Pearl nor Elle finds again for a few more decades.

Back in the caravan, James rolls over onto his side, expecting to see his sister next to him. He startles, realising the caravan is empty, and jumps up with a racing heart. James does not want to be alone. Eyes large, he scans the surroundings of the wilderness out of the caravan window. The smouldering fire pit lies abandoned below his gaze. Searching past the fold-up table with sauce bottles and plates from last night's dinner, through the matches of trees and towards the murky dam, he can feel the blood pounding in his head, and he is clawing at the glass with sweaty palms, intently seeking someone familiar.

Beyond the dam, on the far bank, half-hidden by the trees and vines, he sees them. The back of his mum, arm around his sister. Deep breath. He is not alone.

James watches them through the breath-frosted glass.

CHAPTER 4

Elle—Coming of Age—2002

When Elle was nineteen, she left Australia heartbroken and cashbroken. Excited and naive, Elle and her high school friend Katie flew the long haul to Los Angeles, where they bunked in with Elle's aging grandfather, Vic. The early signs of Alzheimer's disease were present and this annoyed the girls. The old man kept asking them, "Tell me again, how do you know Simon?" And then, wistfully, "He lives so far away."

Elle repeatedly replied, "Gramps, I'm your granddaughter! Simon is my dad. We live in Australia."

Now in his mid-seventies, Vic was confused, as he had not seen his son Simon for over forty years, and here was this blonde Australian girl saying she was his granddaughter. Understandably, the old man was perplexed; however, he showed the girls sincere hospitality and the memorable sights of San Francisco. At times, Elle felt a surge of guilt for encroaching on this old man's space with a self-centred need to know her long-distant grandfather and a self-serving need to have free accommodation in San Francisco. And weirdly, after these feelings subsided, Elle surged with a sense of ownership and responsibility for her dad, who had not stayed in contact with his own father for all these years past. The tendrils of the absence were coated with shame. Elle wondered how a child could not speak to their father for forty-something years, and how they could actually *live* in another country—one on the upside-down side. Nevertheless, here was Elle and her high school friend Katie enjoying the sights of the Golden City and the safe and free accommodation.

After their stay in California, filled with hotdogs and Dr Pepper, the Aussie girls flew to London. Katie and Elle had become close during their last two years of school. They'd bonded over a common maturity that other girls in their year seemed to lack. Katie and Elle talked about books and poetry. Together, they walked their dogs along the beach, and Friday nights were for movies and tea instead of parties and boys. Katie invited Elle to stay with her grandparents in Dubbo one holiday, and Elle was awed by the constant bubble of laughter and affection under the roof of that country home. Later that year, Katie and Elle both got their provisional licences and together they drove to Newcastle to go shopping, Katie ensuring her lights were on because "it's much safer. The other cars can see you better." Fast friends bonded over their equal sensibilities, but Elle did not realise she was walking a tightrope. Her own polarising personality meant she would float between party girl and reading-in-the-library-at-lunch-time girl. She was school captain, top of her classes, and smoked in the bushes between classes. Yet Katie was a good influence on Elle, and for nearly two years, their friendship was founded on respect, deep conversations, and laughter. It was Katie who had saved every cent from working at a department store with her five-year plan and who had known she had to travel for four months before starting a health science degree at university. During an afternoon beach walk, after Elle had confided in her friend that she didn't know what she wanted to do after school, Katie invited her to travel overseas.

"Come," she insisted. "It'll be fun". A month later, Elle had her around-the-world ticket—Singapore, San Fran, Frankfurt, London, Singapore, Sydney—and fifteen hundred dollars in her bank account. The two friends said goodbye to their parents at Sydney Airport. Katie's short, middle-aged parents hugged her, squishing their sparkling, shiny faces and chubby cheeks together like a hamburger, oozing laughter, salty tears, and admiration. Elle had even taken a photo of the happy-sad threesome so she had something to do with her hands, even though Elle now only had twenty-one shots left on the film in her camera. She decided to take another happy shot of her and her mum. In a month's time, the photo would be developed in London, and Elle would glue the smiling portrait into her diary. Many nights, Elle stroked the outline of her mother's face, blowing whispers to her across the oceans and time zones.

Meanwhile, at the airport in Sydney, Elle and Pearl hugged and waved goodbye to each other. Elle conspicuously picked her way to her dad, who had been hovering around the corner at the bookstore. Elle knew Simon did not want to be anywhere near Pearl. Daughter and father politely said goodbye. He handed her a white paper bag.

"Thanks for buying me the book." Elle tucked *To Kill a Mockingbird* under her arm, conscious that *Harry Potter* was in her backpack, and knowing which one she would actually read. Yet, people-pleaser Elle nodded her head and smiled at her dad, reaching up to hug him farewell.

Elle had made her way back to the boarding gate where she'd wrapped her arm around Katie and they'd laughed an excited and nervous cackle together. Looking out across the sea of people all waving goodbye to their loved ones, Elle saw Simon, his tall and lanky figure standing outside of the bookstore where she had left him. She'd cast her gaze ten metres to the right where she smiled at her mum. Katie, on the other hand, had broken out of their embrace and ran back to her parents for a final squeeze and a loud "I'll miss you!"

Elle's mum had smiled and waved weakly, a hint of an apology casting a shadow across her face.

* * *

After the girls had travelled to San Fran and then spent a few weeks together in London seeing all the sights, their paths were about to fork. Katie decided—well, it was always the plan—to travel north to stay with her long-distance family and reconnect with her UK roots. Elle felt a deep craving underneath her loneliness and a sadness in her inability to connect with her American family. Elle was also reckoning with a new-found excitement in her sexual freedom and quiet contentment in her new-found love of gin and tonics. Elle decided to stay in London, in a well-known hostel, where she was able to indulge in cheap drinks at the bar and the transient nature of the people comforted her. She was able to be quirky, outgoing, reckless and uninhibited, and no-one would know she was any different. The invention of herself was just beginning. Elle was shaking free of her nerdy, bookish, introverted self and leaning into the other side of her personality. Katie's sensible friendship, however, did not withstand Elle's crossing of the precipice into the anonymous drunken shadows of London's backpacking culture. They parted ways and Elle jumped headfirst into the raunchy nightlife of the city.

There were boys and men. And girls. There was sex in the toilets, sex in the showers, sex in hotel rooms. The sex was never overly pleasurable for Elle, but the attention and the flippancy of how easily people wanted her body excited her. She thrived from the wanting, the lust, and shied away from second dates. Her sexual confidence masked her detachment from sex.

After nine months of living abroad as a punk-pretty blonde nineteen-year-old Australian working behind a bar and flirting her way through thousands of drunken pool games, she was ready to come home. The hazy drunkenness and the greyness of the concrete city started to close in on her. Elle was longing for green pastures and warm sunshine, for beaches and comfortable rubber thongs. London was damp, cold, hard, and violent. Elle had spent the whole nine months living in a hostel, partying and sleeping in rigid bunk beds with various other foreigners, in smelly dorm rooms and shared, mouldy toilet blocks.

Elle still hadn't acknowledged the reality of her childhood and adolescence—that would not happen for another seven years.

For now, backpacking in London on a shoestring, sex was an act, not a feeling. But still, Elle enjoyed being desired, wanted, fucked. And this she was by people from across the globe. And for a moment in time, Elle believed she was satisfied.

Eventually, the concrete caved in on her blissful view of living in London, which coincided with the death of her half-uncle—if that was what he was. Elle booked her flight home to Sydney. Returning because of the death of a family member was a half-excuse, a little loneliness and a slither of shame for giving up her travels.

The greeting at the airport took place on a balmy autumn morning. Wearing her patchwork skater jeans and black spiked belt, Elle recognised her mum smiling at the back of the crowd as soon as she trotted down the runway. Elle rushed down the ramp, towing her suitcase and heaving her stained and faded backpack, hoping she didn't smell too badly after thirty hours in transit. The people in front of her smiled, *hiiiiiii*ed, and toted balloons and signs and flowers, anxiously celebrating or awaiting the disembarkation of a loved one.

Reaching her mum, Elle started to cry, throwing her arms around Pearl's neck. Mother and daughter stood, wrapped in each other's salty embrace. Pearl must have sensed the changes in Elle—the new-found independence and worldliness she did not have before she left. Pearl did not often worry about Elle, as she was sensible, polite, and kind, if not a little shy, and Elle had always liked following the rules. Elle was a strong advocate for human rights and even though her teenage self-righteousness was mostly annoying, Pearl found it somewhat endearing. Here was adult Elle, nearly twenty, with her pixie hair cut, baggy jeans, leather jewellery, and that god-damn lip piercing. How Pearl wanted to pull that diamond stud from her daughter's lip but instead smiled and told Elle how beautiful she was. Pearl was never one for confrontation, often saying one thing while feeling another.

This was Pearl. A devoted mother, a lover, a matriarch, a runaway wife. And now, standing in the arrivals terminal of Kingsford-Smith Airport, she hugged her adult daughter, pained by the longing she felt to wrap Elle up like a baby and rock her to sleep like she did all those years ago.

It was five minutes after Elle had embraced her mum for the first time in nine months that she finally noticed the young man standing beside her. He was tall and lanky, his head small compared to the stretched limbs of his body. For a moment Elle thought he resembled a needle, with a pin-sized head and skinny, bandy legs. The young man had dark blue piercing eyes and stubble around his chin. His smile was thin-lipped yet warm, familiar yet strange.

James.

He hugged her hard. Whispered in her ear, "Heeeeeey!"

"Oh my god, Jaaaay!" Elle squealed.

Her little brother had grown so tall. The brother who had awkwardly tapped her on the head as she was leaving nine months ago, when he had tousled blonde hair and a squeaky, nearly-thirteen-year-old voice, tired and unaware of what lay ahead, flashed back in her memories. Here he was, puberty blues, gangly and confused, yet her brother nonetheless.

Elle thought back to the message board at the hostel in London where the little post-it notes were stuck for the guests, reminders of the life they'd left back home. Elle had more than a handful of hurried notes: *Elle Bartelle, 21/10/01, Brother called, pls call back.* What did those phone messages mean? James had called her every week. Elle had dismissed the messages, too busy or too broke to call him back from a phone box with an expensive international calling card. She would think of this time abroad for many years to come, and each time her fond memories of freedom and liberty of travelling would be shadowed by guilt and an inability to protect her little brother from the same demon Elle was running from all along. It would be years before she could connect the dots together.

CHAPTER 5

James—Coming of Age—2002

James had felt the emptiness in the house after Elle left the country. At 13, he did not really know what "wandering the world" meant. But her hand-painted purple bedroom door stayed open and sometimes, after school, he would flop down on her bed, pull the mosquito net around the mattress, and stare up at the photos and posters on the ceiling. There she was with four friends, heads together in a star shape lying on the grass, smiling and squinting into the sun; cut-out portraits from parties dressed in satin skirts and midriff tops; group pictures from formals; days at the beach. There was a photo of his sister standing next to a white car with the beach in the background—that was the day she got her licence. James remembers how she picked him up from school, tooting the horn at the gate. He'd blushed and run towards her, feeling so grown up and excited to be her first passenger. Now, he stared up at the numerous band posters like Something for Kate, Third Eye Blind, George, Linkin Park, and Sublime, all curling at the edges and cluttering the ceiling. He wonders what she is listening to now on her cool blue Walkman Dad bought her before she left. He hoped she'd give it to him when she got home. Home is so quiet.

One afternoon, after a particularly emotionally and hormonally charged day of Year 8, ending with Maths and a rowdy bus ride home, he sat in his sister's room between the mattress on the floor and the large wooden tallboy. There was a quote scrawled in lipstick on the mirror: *Some people walk in the rain, others just get wet.*

"Hmm." James scoffed, stomped out of the room, kicked on some boardshorts, and headed for the beach. Along the way, his schoolmate Harley peeled out of a driveway on a rusty pushbike and joined James, and the two blonde-haired kids laughed and farted their way to the waves. At the beach, James and Harley bodysurfed the shore breakers, tumbling and flailing in the foam. Their bodies were buoyed by adrenaline and the innocence of being on the cusp of adolescence and all that would follow.

In the tumultuous, untamed water, James was able to forget about the day at school. The way his Drama teacher—with that furrowed brow—had asked him to stay back at recess, which probably meant James was in trouble again. But after the rest of the rowdy and sweaty teenagers had left the room, James was alone with his teacher, Mr Rogers, who chose to sit down on a greying beanbag and motioned for James to sit on a chair next to him. Hovering, James was undecided about what to do, but he liked Mr Rogers, so after a moment, James swung his backpack to the timber floorboards and straddled the plastic chair with the wobbly leg. Looking intently at James, Mr Rogers clasped his hands, leant forward and pursed his lips.

"How are you going, James?"

Uncomfortable in his gangly teenage body, James squirmed before answering. "Yeah, good, thanks." Hoping the intensity would shift, James forced a wide smile.

"Look, I know you've got a bit going on now that Elle has finished school. You know, she was a great student and I know she looked out for you. I've noticed that some of the other kids are calling you names. Is there something you want to talk about?" Mr Rogers had a round, moon-shaped face and dark, bushy eyebrows. A young teacher, only in his twenties, Mr Rogers was a talented musician and an energetic Drama teacher. James had chosen Drama because he thought the girls would like him, and it was better than the alternative of Physical Education, which was full of the footy boys who were so much bigger than James. Being only one of two boys in the Drama class, James figured he was safer there, and anyway, he was funny and the girls laughed with him when he performed and improvised, which was better than the footy boys laughing at him.

"Um, I don't really care about what they are saying," James said, somewhat honestly.

Mr Rogers leaned back in his chair and began a monologue about his own personal journey through the performing arts as a young man and something about his dad not wanting him to pursue Drama teaching as a career because it was "for poofs". James listened to snippets of what his teacher said, but it was hard for James to concentrate. The word *poof* kept echoing in his mind, and it made him squirm.

Mr Rogers finished his speech by assuring James he had "a natural talent, and you are a valued member of the class. If there is anything you need, just ask." Mr Rogers looked like an eager puppy dog, with wide eyes framed with big ears and a wobbly mid-section. Politely, James offered a smile and a nod, muttered "thanks", and stood up, collecting his bag.

"Hey, James," Mr Rogers called just as James reached the door. "You and Elle both have amazing imaginations. You must have had a really exciting childhood!"

"Um, yeah, I guess." And James slinks out of the doorway into the glaring sunshine and clamorous crowded quadrangle. He intentionally pushes away thoughts of his childhood and finds a quiet corner to sit in and unwrap his Vegemite sandwich.

Two months later, James would buy his first boat—a tinny—with the cash he had been saving from working as a trolley collector at the local grocery store. A slippery and slightly rusty 3.3 m tinny, equipped with a Wilson eight-foot cast net, a nine-horse-power motor, two oars, two mouldy lifejackets he would never wear, an anchor, and two fishing rod holders. James and a handful of his mates frothed over the boat. Each Friday afternoon, they could be heard motoring down the river, yahooing and slandering one another. They would pull up on one of the isolated, scattered islands to camp, fish, and experiment with pot. They talked about girls and bodyboarding, fishing, and "remember when" tales of practical jokes, bloody accidents that left scars, acts of vandalism, and boyish bravado-isms. James could feel the world opening to him. He felt free in the salty air and the laughter around him. For now, life was easy.

CHAPTER 6

James—Roommates—2006

It is 2006, and Elle and James have decided to rent a unit together at Gosford. It's a tidy, two-bedroom split-level unit up the hill from the train station and a short walk to the town centre. Elle is twenty-three, has not met Adrian yet, and James has recently finished high school, just scraping by with a below-average ATAR, having chosen surfing and fishing over homework and assessment deadlines. He knows his mum is disappointed with him, even though she would never say so. He knows his teachers expected more of him, considering how academic his sister was. It's hard for him not to feel shitty, but he pretends he doesn't care.

James finished school with a couple of friends—namely other larrikins who enjoyed sport and the ocean. Together, James and two mates travelled between Sydney, Newcastle, and the Central Coast, couch-surfing between friends' places and randoms they met at a party or in the water. After a year of this lifestyle, Elle invited James to move in with her. He appreciated that his sister could see he was drowning and that she wanted to help.

Originally, James planned to move to Sydney and live with his dad. Simon lived in a trendy harbour-side unit with great views located atop the ferry station. Both Elle and James loved the nights out in the city, clubbing at Kings Cross and then catching a yellow ferry back to Simon's place, usually while he was away overseas or interstate for work. When in town, Simon would take Elle and James out for dinner, buy expensive wine, leave a generous tip, and afterwards they would find a pub to play pool, drink whiskey, and smoke cigarettes. Well, the boys would drink whiskey while Elle sipped a gin and tonic. They had fun times, but always with a drink and a smoke in hand. Simon's life impressed James. It always had. From when they were just kids and would catch the train to Sydney every second weekend, James had idolised his father. Simon would let them eat all the junk food that Pearl would never buy. He took them to Timezone, the cinema, Luna Park, Cirque du Soleil shows, fast food places, and fluorescent skate rinks. Simon seemed to have endless money, but Elle could see the Amex card. She didn't ask her dad for things like James did. James wanted the shoes and the toys and the food; Elle wanted Simon's approval and validation.

While Simon was living in a bachelor pad in North Sydney after he first separated from Pearl, Elle remembers Simon teaching her and James—then only six—to play poker. Her dad had a large jar of silver coins, and he would let them have their own piles of *real money*. The three of them would play cards for hours. James hoarded his twenty-cent pieces and waited until they went to George Street where he would frivolously feed the coins into the slots at Timezone. Elle, on the other hand, would feed the coins back into the glass jar from which they came.

This fast and consumerist lifestyle was what James wanted when he finished school and escaped the mid-north coast and its sleepy beachside vibe. He could not wait to pack his bag, say "fuck you" to the stragglers from his year who didn't rush away to a trade or uni, and live his best life in Sydney. Doing what, he wasn't sure—but he knew it would be fun.

This could have been the start of the many disappointments in James's life. He had such high expectations of leaving his adolescence and entering the glamour and freedom of adulthood. High expectations of leaving behind the shame of his experiences, the shitty high school days. James asked his dad if he could move in with him, and quite abruptly, and with unusual honesty, Simon said, “No. I’m too busy. I’ve just met someone, and I don’t want to ruin what we have so far.”

And then James started drinking.

Elle notices the drinking now that they live together. It is a Tuesday night, and they decide to walk down the hill to Gosford RSL Club. Elle is studying at university while working at a pub by night, and James has a part-time job at an RSL club at the other end of the Central Coast. Their hospitality working hours mean their “weekends” fall mid-week, and this particular Tuesday night starts off as many others had. They walk down the hill, laughing and telling stories about their week. They pass the hospital and football stadium, arrive at the club, and flash their identification cards at the bouncer manning the automatic door.

Inside the venue, the fluorescent lights bear down and the poker machines dance and sing and jingle. James orders the first round of the drinks and they play a game of blackjack. Between them, they don’t have much money, but the sense of freedom, lack of foresight, and youth, all mixed with alcohol, influence their decision to gamble whatever disposable income they have. After thirty dollars is lost and two drinks are drunk, Elle calls it a night. On the way out, James stops and buys a bottle of Southern Comfort “for later”.

Back at their unit, Elle and James have one drink of Southern Comfort mixed with some flat lemonade Elle found hiding at the back of the fridge and smoke a cigarette on the balcony.

“Goodnight,” Elle yawns. “I gotta be in class at nine tomorrow. Ugh.” She saunters off up the steps, cleans her teeth, and falls into bed.

James stubs out his cigarette and sits in the darkness on the verandah. Above the neighbours’ building, he can see twinkling lights from the telecommunication towers and the high-rises perched on the hillside. He hears the rumble of traffic below and a TV playing a game show in a unit above. He thinks about going to bed and suddenly the memories shuffle through him like a serrated knife through the femur of a sow. The grinding is soft at first—small glimpses of hands, saliva, darkness. James shudders in the inky night air. He is tired, yet the idea of sleep slips away from him in terror. He knows he won't be able to fall asleep. He will feel the shame, hear the groans, taste the blood. As James sits in the darkness, another cigarette in his hand, he feels the clawing, incessant pawing of the addiction. He has had three drinks. It's time for bed.

Instead, in the dark, he pours another Southern Comfort.

* * *

Elle is woken during the night by a banging. She climbs out of bed and kicks on her slippers.

Downstairs, she hears the song "Rainbow Stylin'" by The Similou echoing its beats around James's room. There he is, dancing to the rhythm and throwing a bottle artistically in the air, twirling, catching, and spinning. James majestically bends his knees, bounces his blonde head, tosses the sparkling bottle, catches it with his left hand, the bottle balancing on his slender fingertips, waits for the count, feels the beat, then tosses it up into the air, attempts to land the bottle on his right shoulder but it rolls down his back and, *bang*, shatters into a million little pieces on the tiles. But that is not what upsets Elle.

What upsets her is the fact that it's an empty bottle.

It's an empty 750 mL bottle of Southern Comfort, it's two o'clock on a Wednesday morning, and James is nineteen years old. What Elle does not know is that it has been one year since James's older brother took him to a nightclub at Kings Cross. That story will come later.

CHAPTER 7

Elle—Just Surviving Her Twenties—2009

After returning from her travels, Elle survived her early twenties with passion and impulsivity. She backpacked along the East Coast with a friend from Italy. She worked in dive bars flirting with older men. There was a stint working as a "parts tart" driving car spare parts to local mechanics, and she would be singing too loudly to Blink-182, wearing too-short cut-off denim shorts, throwing her cigarette butts out the window of the delivery van, but earning money and paying her bills on time. She still loved to read, devouring books about fantastical creatures and true stories of remarkable women. And she spent hours sketching with charcoal, making art that was thoughtful and detailed, yet there was a darkness creeping in. Elle's optimism had waned, and dark shadows were cast across her poetry and artworks. The music she listened to had become louder, angrier, sadder. Something was clawing at her, and she tried desperately to keep it at bay with alcohol, sex, and the occasional bump of speed or coloured pills of ecstasy.

Elle fell in and out of love everywhere she went and unapologetically broke up with every guy she sort-of-maybe cared for. She started, and eventually finished, her degree in teaching, never really losing her passion for reading, poetry, and performance.

At one impulsive stage, having just turned twenty-five, she even married a guy—Adrian. They met while she was working at a local tavern. He came in and smiled, and the rest was a whirlwind love affair fuelled by passion and lust. He was twelve years her senior, and she was intrigued by his maturity and his love of music and travel. After six months, they went to New Zealand and hired a campervan, travelling the South Island, hiking and drinking red wine around a fire. Adrian had an exuberant spirit, fiery and energetic. It was at midnight on New Year's Eve at Queenstown, on the banks of the river and underneath the light of the fireworks, that he proposed to her. Elle remembered feeling embarrassed at first and desperately wanted him to stand up. She looked around, anxious about someone seeing the monumental proposal. A few people cheered from the shadows and, motivated by the attention, she quickly said, "Yes; get up, just get up. Yes." Hugging him in the darkness, she thought of a song by Taylor Swift.

Three months later, Elle and Adrian eloped in Las Vegas, walking down the aisle to the charming song "What Shall We Do with the Drunken Sailor?" Needless to say, this relationship did not last long—about eighteen months—and maybe the wedding song was a metaphor for their marriage. After the ceremony—as exciting and unique as it was, followed by a month of cocaine-fuelled escapades through LA, New York, and San Fran—Elle had grown restless. Back home in Australia as newlyweds, they rented an old home in the coal mining town of Mayfield in Newcastle, and Adrian used his carpentry skills to renovate it, letting in more light to the windowless home. While Adrian showed his affection towards her at every opportunity and insisted on spending quality time together—not even wanting her to go to the supermarkets without him—and showered her with words of affirmation, Elle began feeling caged. Adrian's repetitive catchphrases made her cringe; his harsh judgments of others made her recoil. Suddenly, now they were married and living together, she was getting to know him. Realising she should have known him better before she married him, Elle was angry at herself. Now she was married, her lack of independence made her feel nauseous. In the house, she felt boxed in. In the relationship, she felt controlled, unhappy. She cried at night and listened to the language loop in her mind. *I don't want to be a wife. I don't want to be a wife.*

Not long after these thoughts had taken root, Adrian lost his temper—not for the first time, but the first time in the public eye—at a backyard party.

It was Anzac Day, and Elle and Adrian had ridden their hipster cruiser pushbikes down to the local hotel. After a few beers and games of pool, Elle started inviting people to their place, saying they would host a party. Adrian was reluctant but agreeable, and so Elle excitedly led twenty-something twenty-somethings down the back laneway to their renovated two-bedroom Federation-style mining home on Awabakal Country.

In the kitchen, Elle was seated atop the kitchen bench, looking across at the sea of people gathered, staggering, undulating in the lounge room. Adrian had turned on his ridiculously expensive decks and someone—Damo?—was playing amateur DJ. Elle asked Sophie for a cigarette. Elle had stopped smoking a few months earlier, due to Adrian's incessant pestering. He was studying to be a doctor and had switched from being cocaine-cool to cacao-kale-smoothie cool, and Elle wasn't sure she had kept up with the changes.

"Thanks, Soph," Elle said and smiled as she lit the smoke and took a long drag, swinging her legs to a Flight Facilities song.

Suddenly, Adrian was between Elle's legs, his sweaty forehead pressed against hers, and his rapid breath reeking of rum. Adrian snarled, grabbed her hands, and twisted her fingers backwards till she dropped the cigarette.

"Hey, ow, stop!" Elle screeched.

He didn't stop. Adrian's eyes were dark and flickering as he glared at her, bending her fingers back so forcefully she was sure her fingers would snap like one, two, three, four, matchsticks inside his hairy grip. Elle, whilst not moved by surprise, was enraged at his audacity and she swung at him with her legs, hard. Adrian launched backwards, which gave her enough time to jump off the island bench and stomp out the back door, where more people were drinking, laughing, and smoking, and had not, thankfully, seen the exchange. Elle was a little drunk and a little confused by what just happened.

"Hey, Claire, can I have a smoke, please?" Adrian had twisted the last one from Elle's spindly fingers, and now her anger and frustration fuelled her vengeance. She would smoke again. Claire passed her a smoke and Elle lit the cigarette but was not able to inhale, as she was knocked sideways out of the chair and onto the concrete patio. Around her, she heard squeals and surprised *ahhhhs*. Flailing, Elle was face to face with the cold ground but fear and muscle memory forced her to her feet, screaming. A hand grabbed her by the throat, forcing her backwards, upwards, against something hard—the Colorbond fence. Elle couldn't see much at all other than the black silhouettes of bodies and the bright fluorescent sensor light flickering behind them. Elle could feel the tightness around her throat, and she tried to scream.

It didn't last long. In three heartbeats, Adrian released her, and Elle crumpled to the ground again, soon heaved up by not one, but three girlfriends, cussing and cooing and growling, embracing her from all sides and pulling her down the side of the house, through the laneway, out into the quiet street and away from the party. Away from Adrian. They held her and carried her all the way to Claire's house. Here they wrapped her in a blanket, gave her a cup of green tea, and told her she was safe. Elle felt such deep gratitude, coupled with searing shame and endless embarrassment.

Now, everyone knew what a mistake she had made, and the shame seeped deeper into her veins.

CHAPTER 8

James—Surviving His Twenties—2009

Before the intense night of the incident over a cigarette, when things were sort of okay between Eleanor and Adrian, James came to stay with them in Newcastle. James had been a little lost the past few years since leaving school. Elle had tried to help him out while they rented a unit at Gosford together, but James had trouble keeping up with the rent and they started arguing. Elle realised she didn't want to ruin their relationship so she suggested they break the lease. James agreed, although he felt abandoned by another family member. He reached out to a mate from school who was living in North Sydney and he agreed James could couch surf there for a while until something else came up. James managed to hold a few different jobs, working in sweaty bars, labouring on hot job sites, and moving between friends' homes and Pearl's place. It had been a while since he had seen his sister, as she had moved further north to finish uni. And she had married that deadshit guy Adrian. But Elle seemed desperate to see him, her little-big brother, and she persisted with weekly phone calls and frequent text messages. James often ignored her calls, as he had little to say.

"Come, stay, Jay!" she begged him. Yet James always managed to sound despondent and made excuses about it being too far to travel.

Finally, after James had quit yet another bar job because "the manager was a dick", he agreed to visit her and Adrian in their small home cloaked with coal dust from the mining port. When James finally arrived, parking his rusting white van in the cul-de-sac, he smiled brightly at his big sister, realising at that moment just how much he had missed her. Elle hugged and squeezed her little-big brother, and James melted into her embrace. His depressive feelings lately were taking their toll, along with struggling to pay his share of the rent at a place in North Sydney that he shared with friends of friends. He felt like they were judging him because he couldn't pay the bills on time. There was that, and *some other stuff.*

Elle and James smoked cigarettes on the balcony and drank mojitos. Pat the Dog, Adrian's fiercely loyal cattle dog, showed off all his tricks—sit, drop, stay, play dead, hide, stand, dance—and then gleefully chased the ball for hours until the sun set. James, Adrian, and Elle laughed at silly YouTube clips about animal antics. They played indie-electronic tunes on the DJ decks and watched back-to-back episodes of the TV series *Lost*. Afterwards, James showed them his card tricks and entertained them with his showcase of jokes, always one to please a crowd. He could charm a bitter sixty-seven-year-old grandma, a pimply twelve-year-old kid or a suave twenty-eight-year-old car dealer. He had the swag; he had the yarn; he had the charm. Elle admired all the strengths in James that she herself lacked. Together, they were the perfect seesaw: unbalanced yet balanced all the same.

It was the third morning of his visit when Elle called out to James for breakfast. She had sliced up a rainbow of fresh fruit and topped it with Greek yoghurt and some hemp seeds. Elle loved riding her bike to the local farmer's markets and filling her backpack with raw goods. She was proud of her new-found love of fresh, vibrant food, and was excited to share it with her brother. After all, she thought he looked like he needed some nourishment.

"James!" Elle shouted through the timber bedroom door, knocking at the same time.

No answer.

Adrian had already locked himself in the study to complete another tutorial for his medical degree. No doubt he had his noise-cancelling headphones on and was frowning deeply into his coffee cup.

"Jay?" Elle whispered and felt her skin go cold. She pushed open the door. "Fuck."

The room was empty. The bed was a mess and there were clothes strewn across the floor. It smelt mildly of dirty socks and stale fart. Elle plucked her phone from her pocket and called her brother. It went straight to voicemail. Her heart started to race a little more.

She stumbled backwards out of the room, a few steps forward along the hallway and opened the front door, heaving herself cross-legged onto the daybed that Adrian had built her so she could read books in the afternoon sun. But Elle hardly used it for that, and instead, it had become her smoking corner. She took a deep draw on her ciggy and looked out across the street. *Where could he be? Why did he leave? Should she tell Adrian? Maybe. Actually, no. Not yet.* Another draw. Exhaling a plume of grey smoke. Her face flushed, her nerves pulsing. She looked at her phone: 8:13 am. Elle called James again and again, but it went through to his voicemail each time. She sighed.

At 10:27am, James barrelled through the front door, wet.

"Oh my God, James. What the fuck?" Elle met him in the hallway, hands on her hips and lips pursed.

He smiled; no, he grimaced.

"Aw, Ez, so funny, I've had an epic night with my mate Dave." He swayed a little and his pupils were dilated.

"Dave? Who's Dave?"

"Dave! My mate from Sydney! Yeah, he called, and I was, like, 'hey, yeah, for sure man, I'll be there!'" James pushed past Elle in the tiny hallway and loped into the lounge room, where he collapsed cheerfully onto a recliner, kicking his legs out and clasping his hands behind his head. Elle glared at him.

After a moment, James realised his sister was pissed. He caught the scorned look on her face, the ripple of skin puckered between her brows. The wild adventure from the night before seemed like a long time ago, but James had the urge to cheer up his boring sister with one of his entertaining stories.

"But why are you wet? And it's ten in the morning!"

"Aw, shit." James grabbed at his clothes as though it were the first time he'd noticed the dampness. He stood up and stripped off his soggy shirt, tossing it onto the floor.

"Aw, yeah, that's right. We jumped off the bridge! It was so fucking funny, Ez, you should have seen us! It was like, pitch-black and I dared Dave to jump. I didn't think he would, but you know Dave—he just, like, did it! So then I had to, too. I didn't even know if there were like, fucking boats or shit in the water. But I did it." He giggled a strangely boyish sound.

"No, I actually don't know Dave, James." She was annoyed. So what if he had sneaked out, not told her, got high, and jumped off a bridge, for fucks' sake. Elle was being all hoity-toity and it was ruining James's high. She needed to stop worrying about him. He wasn't a little kid anymore.

Just then, Adrian unlocked the study door and he stood looming in the doorway, an empty and stained coffee cup dangling from his hand.

"What the fuck, Eleanor?" Adrian roared at her when they were alone in the bedroom. Elle had sunk onto the bed, still in her pyjamas even though it was late afternoon.

"You said it would be fine, and it's not!" he hurled at her. She covered her face with her hands and could feel the tears stinging her eyes. She was so exhausted.

"I know," she whispered. "I know I said that." The truth was, Elle always wanted it to be fine. Each time, in her heart, she thought James was getting better. And each time she was left feeling even more deflated than the last time.

CHAPTER 9

James—Recruitment—2008

Each time James visited his sister, he left feeling less buoyed than the last time. Where she used to laugh easily and share banter, now she looked at him with concern and worry, and James felt the coolness enter his blood. He couldn't seem to shake the unease. Depleted again, he drove back home to North Sydney and lay on his roommate's faded corduroy lounge because, other than his bed and clothes, James did not own anything in the shitty house. Hands behind his head, stretched out on his back, he stared up at the paint peeling from the ceiling and let his thoughts swirl around his mind. The room was dull and musky. The coffee table in the middle of the room was overflowing with ashtrays, lighters, and empty DVD covers.

Eventually, James heard the front door unlock, closely followed by a set of footsteps along the timber floorboards and into the lounge room, stopping right behind James's head. He closed his eyes.

"Hey," said Harley.

"Hey," yawned James, pretending he had been napping instead of lying there in a catatonic state for nearly two hours.

"I got the green." Harley tossed a stick of foil at James's stomach, which made James sit up, smiling.

And for the rest of the afternoon, James and Harley smoked cones through a blackened glass bong. And for the rest of the afternoon, James's thoughts evaporated into the emptiness.

The next morning, James was tired and hungry. He checked the time and realised he had his appointment in just over an hour. After showering and pulling on old jeans, scuffed trainers, and a cleanish shirt, which he sprayed with deodorant, he made a peanut butter sandwich and searched for his phone, wallet, and keys. Eventually, James found himself out in the street trying to unlock his car. The sun was blaring down and he squinted into the sky. *Fuck*, he mumbled, about nothing in particular other than in response to the day itself.

Two months earlier, after quitting his job as a bartender at the Cricketers Arms because his boss was riding his back about being on time, even though parking in the city is a bitch, James couldn't pay the rent. He wallowed for a few days, smoking extra cones and drinking vinegary wine out of a foil bag, and then he called his dad to ask for help. Unsurprisingly, Simon gave him fifty bucks to help buy groceries and a train pass. James needed more than fifty bucks, so he called his mum. Pearl transferred a hundred dollars into his account and James was able to give his roommate half of this towards the rent. But while he was explaining the predicament to Pearl, she suggested that he take a proactive step into a career. *Labouring? A trade? Go to TAFE?* He scoffed. He felt judged. He felt tired. All of his teenage energy and vibrancy was sapped by the let-down of city life and adulthood. Being an adult sucked and James was terrible at it.

He called his cousin Mick, who was living in Darwin as a fresh army graduate. Mick had always been a mate to James. Despite the age difference, Mick had understood James's sense of humour and together they shared many yarns about various comedians, adventure TV shows, new craft beers, and stupidly funny antics of their mates. James looked up to his older cousin and loved to hear about his travels abroad. During their phone call, James started to imagine his own life in the army. Maybe the rigid structure would be good for him. And anyway, he wouldn't have to pay rent or cook. He had heard the food at the mess was substantial and the recruits never went hungry. In between topics, James sideways mentioned to Mick that he was thinking of signing up. He hesitated, but Mick smiled broadly down the phone line and cheered. "Fuck yeah, man!" he shouted. James felt the smile rippling through the fibre optic lines, along the electromagnetic waves where the puppy grin connected to his own cheeks, his teeth bursting through lips with joy and relief. Now that he had said it out loud—*I want to sign up*—he felt the weight of boredom, darkness, and purposelessness lifted from his shoulders. James breathed deeply and laughed along with Mick.

So James got off the phone, trotted his way to a local internet cafe two blocks from his North Sydney dilapidated house, and searched for the enrolment details on the Defence Force website. A flutter of excitement churned in his stomach. He had not felt this feeling since he was in Year 11, when he was first planning on leaving school and living with his old man in Sydney. Remembering how that plan did not come to fruition, he momentarily stopped searching and caught a wispy breath in his chest. He rubbed his neck and looked around the cafe at the people with direction and determination and connections. James felt a longing to be one of these people. To feel like he belonged.

Returning to the computer screen, with the list of potential careers under subheadings, the word "artillery" jumped out at him: *Be part of the team that sets up, aims, and fires one of the Army's most powerful weapons in a role full of camaraderie and ongoing opportunities.*

Imagining firing those weapons deep into the face of the enemy, James envisioned his revenge. He visualised his victory. He clicked on the link that read: *Apply*.

* * *

Today is his interview. James is trying to get his key into the driver's side door while squinting at the brightness of the day. "Fuck," he mumbles again. He is tired after smoking cones with his roommate all night. Two months ago, when James first made the call to the Defence Force, he was keen to get his life on track. He was sick of living week to week on a measly minimum wage, partying with unreliable friends and smoking away the boredom. James was eager to join the recruits with the exciting prospect of being the guy who builds and fires weapons. On the phone, the intake lady was kind and reassuring. Darla, that was her name. She gave James a list of all the documents he needed to supply, along with the health and fitness requirements. Darla also invited him to attend an information session at the city office where he could hear about the different job opportunities and have any questions answered. "Thanks," James said, "but I'm pretty keen on joining the artillery recruits."

Darla said something that made him think of his mum, and then she bade him good luck and said farewell. James was buoyed and elated at the prospect of being an army recruit. He was eager for the gruelling fitness regime and knew his scrawny limbs would bulk up if only he had the right trainer and adequate nutrition. He desperately needed to get out of the miserable house in North Sydney and out into the real, colourful world. James knew the army was the answer to his boredom and lack of direction; it was his saviour from self-destructive behaviour. Yes, two months ago he was keen as bloody mustard.

Today, however, James is lacking that enthusiasm. He has had two months of smoking, drinking, surviving on two-minute noodles, and not doing much else. James has lost even more weight; his limbs are too long for his body.

While trying to jam his key into the lock, the phone vibrates in his pocket. It's Pearl.

Good luck today, reads the text. And James smiles because his mum remembered. And he smiles because he *is* going to go to the interview, he *is* going to put the final pieces into the puzzle, and he *is* going to be a hero.

Thanks, James types. *I'm running late.*

* * *

The first, second, and third recruitment interviews all go well. So well that, today, James is leaving for the training camp at Kapooka. Perhaps it will all work out after all, James considers, as he dresses in his state-issued camo and heaves his duffel bag onto his back. Glancing one last time at the North Sydney house, its peeling paint, graffitied walls, curling carpet, and decaying furniture, James leaves the darkness and makes his way to the city of Newcastle. With every breath, he is promising himself a fresh start. Health, fitness, no drinking, no pot.

At the registration centre, other young faces speckle the waiting room, their loved ones in civilian clothes grasping hands and shoulders and wiping away tears. Pearl stands close to James, elbow to elbow, as they wait for his name to be called. Elle is there, too, sitting on a velvet bench seat underneath a large, glossy poster of three army recruits tracking through long grass and text that reads *This is belonging*. James clicks his fingers nervously and scans the other faces, searching for possible companionship. His mum makes small talk—"Do you have your toothbrush? I saw the weather is cooling down in Wagga Wagga"—and he nods in all the right places. When his name is called, James shuffles through the crowd and registers his attendance. The clerk checks his bag and his uniform. He fills in a document. Signs his name. Ticks the correct boxes. Shuffles back to say his goodbyes.

Elle squeezes him tightly. So tightly that James wonders if she is crying. Her hair smells like tobacco, and James has an urge to smoke then remembers that he is now an ex-smoker. He stands tall in his uniform, pride surging through his body. He will miss his sister, his mum, and his mates, but he is fucking excited to be escaping this shit-hole.

"Sis," he says, pulling away from her hug, "I'll be fine. See you in three months. You won't even recognise me, I'll be so buff." Elle scoffs at her little-big brother, with his small head and gangly limbs.

Pearl embraces him next, warm and soft. James nearly cries. Nearly.

It's time to board the bus. The other recruits are slowly embarking and people are waving and dabbing at their eyes with tissues. James follows the line of uniforms and climbs up the steps onto the coach. He walks down the aisle and finds a seat next to the window.

Outside, on the concrete footpath, Pearl and Elle watch his silhouette, and they wave, expecting him to turn and look at them.

The bus pulls away. James does not look back. If he did, he would have seen Pearl crying.

CHAPTER 10

Elle—Morphing—2008

Her little brother seemed too young and too innocent to be holding a gun. It was as though he had not even started shaving, and watching him board the military bus dressed in uniform made Elle feel conflicted. On the one hand, she was proud of her brother. On the other hand, she was deeply worried for him. Regardless, Elle waved goodbye as the bus pulled away and she hugged her tearful mother, holding her tightly. James was headed for the intensive training program at Kapooka and she would not speak with her brother for eight weeks.

Having recently returned from another year abroad, this time to Namibia, Elle was maturing and her self-righteousness was at its peak. With a bleeding heart on her sleeve, Elle had taken a year's volunteer work in the destitute town of Mondesa, outside of the coastal, touristy, German-influenced town of Swakopmund. The devastating historical hangover from apartheid was evident in the separation of the people existing in neighbouring suburbs, primarily based on colour and class. As an Anglo-Saxon Westerner, Elle, and two other Canadian teachers, all in their mid-twenties, were offered the luxury of a three-bedroom home by the seaside, with electricity and running water and within walking distance of fully stocked supermarkets. Elle and her new-found roommates enjoyed living in the township. Contrastingly, the young Namibian students who attended the school merely four kilometres from the city centre lived in ramshackle shanties—built with discarded tin sheets—that sat huddled together in dust bowls. Nicknamed the DRC, there was no running water or electricity or fully stocked supermarkets. There were dingy *shebeens* and desperate prostitutes. There were undernourished women who believed the human body had two livers. There were iniquitous men who believed that the only cure for AIDS was to have sex with a virgin.

The not-for-profit school where Elle volunteered as a teacher aimed to give selected, gifted students who showed potential to succeed the much-needed support to achieve a meaningful education. The students would walk, barefoot, to the rented space at the lacklustre local library, and they would share plastic seats at wooden desks crammed into a tiny space. Elle was in awe of how these wide-eyed children soaked up all of the tuition offered despite being hungry and sickly. The gratitude, willingness, and resilience of these little people would become a powerful memory for Elle, and a reminder of how strong the human spirit can truly be.

It was Lance who suggested Elle take the opportunity of a year abroad in Namibia. Her older brother, full of self-importance and bravado, encouraged her to apply, and he even offered to fund her flights. Elle, feeling the niggling sensation of the darkness and the power Lance held over her, was eager to flee the country again. Flighty and unsettled, Elle could not yet articulate why she felt the need to adventure far from her homeland. Nor could she recognise the subconscious obligation to advocate for other vulnerable young people.

The year abroad in Namibia was formative. Confronting, challenging, humbling, and rewarding. Elle was determined to find ways to use her skills as a teacher to bridge the gap between poverty and education in her waking life. She would, in the future, become a teacher of special education and would work in remote parts of Western Australia with First Nations students.

After a year away, she has returned home, living in a rented apartment on Darkinjung Country. Tonight is Lance's thirtieth birthday party, and Elle is trying on dresses. She has kept her hair short, scruffy, and pointy. August is cold, and once she is satisfied with her outfit, Elle slides into boots, grabs an oversized second-hand woollen coat, and heads towards the train station.

Arriving at the venue, a well-lit hotel in the northern suburbs of Sydney, Elle is met by a raucous tribe of Lance's companions, a mixture of his old school friends and new work colleagues. When Lance first moved to Sydney to live with his dad, it was Simon who introduced his eldest son to the expanding and popular world of technology, computer programming, and information processing. Simon had been working in advertising for a major tech company and used his professional credit to secure Lance an entry-level job in the same building. Within three years, Lance—clever and manipulative Lance—outpaced Simon's skill set and was promoted to a leadership role. Shortly after, Simon was made redundant. Lance's ego grew larger than his crooked nose, and the money in his bank account afforded him the luxury of paying any price for whatever he desired.

Tonight Lance is celebrating himself and Elle feels nauseous to be in his company. She feels like a fraud being among the many who adore him. Loud and obnoxious, drunk and high, the partygoers play pool, feed notes into the poker machines, and suck on cigarettes. Elle fills her unsettled belly with red wine until she no longer cares what people think of the "little sister". The hazy drunkenness offers her a much-needed freedom to relax.

Many years later, Elle will remember this night as the last evening she ever pretended she did not remember what Lance did to her. The next time she sees Lance, Elle's repressed fury is palpable.

CHAPTER 11

James—Deployment—April, 2015

The noise of the helicopter out-screams the pounding heartbeats and chainsaw thoughts of the regiment crew hunched on the vibrating bench seats, gripping their weapons and holding back their tears. Some have tears of exhilaration, some of fear. Some, like James, have tears from the dust circling and infiltrating their goggles. Down below, James can make out the sparse desert landscape. The sun is setting, which makes the sand look like a murky lake in the dimming light. Somewhere in the distance of the Uruzgan province splays the Tarin Kowt Army Base Camp that will be James's home for the next eight months.

Just a few years ago, he survived the gruelling instruction at Kapooka—the "home of the soldier"—and he was deployed to Adelaide shortly after. There he trained and worked his arse off, waiting for the call-to-arms when he could really prove his worth. In between partying with his comrades on the few days a month he had off, he would be sucking down Valium and clonazepam to mask his social anxiety. No-one knew about his anxiety, not even his family. It was a feeling he couldn't shake these past few years, and after speaking with the army psych for six and a half minutes, he was prescribed the meds and now James takes them like lollies. Feeling the old boredom from his days living in North Sydney creeping under his skin, James was feeling self-destructive again. He was itching to be deployed and to have the choice of taking drugs dissipated by distance and heavy-handed authority. Eventually, the official letter appeared, and James was summoned to be part of the third phase of Operation Slipper in Afghanistan.

Now the day has arrived and the battalion members are awaiting the drop from the helicopter. They have spent hours preparing for this day. Simulations, AI testing, real-life combat. Everyday civilians turned into capable, resourceful, and heavily armed forces. Everyday young men turned into an emotionless, compliant, and robotic force.

James looks around at his battalion, nicknamed C-RAM, an acronym for counter-rocket/artillery/ mortar. They would all have their part to play in the war against the Taliban, but this deployment was part of a reconstruction task force, whereby its mission was to conduct protected restoration operations in the remote areas of the province as part of a broader Dutch-led task force.

Gunner James Bartelle was bored shitless during the two weeks of briefing sessions they had back at Hampstead Barracks on Australian soil. He felt like he was at school again, listening to the presenter drone on about the history of the war in Afghanistan and the purpose of Operation Slipper. James would have preferred to be lugging a fully loaded backpack through mud and rain in the middle of the Adelaide winter than sitting in that auditorium hearing buzz words like "reconciliation", "reconstruction", and "cultural empowerment". *Put a weapon in my hand,* he thought, *then I'll show you empowerment.*

James is now mentally preparing himself for eight months underground in his new role as a member of the ADF. He was told he'd be working three-hour shifts around the clock with little time for anything else. In the dark underground cell, James will be watching a computer screen and searching for any enemy aircraft. If, by chance, the enemy aircraft is sighted, all he needs to do is press a button to alert the powers that be. Otherwise, James is looking at a screen with very little movement. In the dark underground cell, James will have plenty of time to think. Plenty of time to remember.

The sun has nearly set and the lights of the helicopter flicker green and then red. The bright beam at the front of the chopper lights the way for the pilot. A glaring cone of power. Here they come, the glorious Australian Army.

Prior to being deployed, James and a selection of other artillery specialists were flown to Oklahoma, where they were trained in the use of the counter-rocket, artillery, mortar intercept Land-based Phalanx Weapon System (LPWS). The beast of a weapon was mounted on a commercial thirty-five-tonne semi-trailer for land-based operations and weighed a ginormous twenty-six thousand kilograms. It needed a crew of four human operators, and James was on one of these teams being trained. Over the month he spent in the United States, he learnt that the M61A1 20 mm Gatling gun was capable of onboard target acquisition and fire control with a sustained four thousand, five hundred rounds per minute. It fired rounds designed to self-destruct beyond two thousand metres to minimise potential collateral damage. It was also clever enough to be capable of an integrated search-and-track radar detection to engage with a wide range of indirect threats. This made James feel a little safer, although the power of the rocket was greater than anything else he had controlled before.

In the desert, as the men practised, they drove, carried, constructed, and fired the weapon. The training was intense and the expectations were high. Each member had to be faster and more efficient than the last soldier, pulling their pieces of the weapon and initialising the infrastructure. Blasting the rocket into the sandy dunes, and witnessing it self-destruct at two thousand metres was a rush the men felt for years to come. During the training, they hastily took cover, disarmed the weapon, and continued through to the next checkpoint. Repeat. The drills were hard on their bodies. Once, while heaving an LPWS barrel from the ground, James felt a sudden deep burn scald his shoulder and pulsate down his arm. He screamed in pain and dropped the barrel onto the sand. There was a flurry of movement from his comrades, unwrapping the uniform from his body and seeing the dislocated shoulder popped clean out of its cavity. James still winces when he remembers how Sapper Ted Robinson shunted his shoulder back into place and directed him, sternly, to "keep moving" through the terrain.

Now, James rubs his shoulder as he feels the helicopter hesitate. Slowing, the pilot pulls the aircraft to a steady hover, the beacon of light intensifying on a sandy flat down below. Up ahead, at least five hundred metres away, James can see the shadowy boxes of site offices and metal shipping containers that James imagines will be the sleeping quarters. Military wire is draped around the building blocks, marking the territory of the Tarin Kowt Army Base. The dust is everywhere, up James's nose, in his ears, between his fingers. He rubs his neck and sniffs, smelling the petrol fumes of the chopper mixed with acrid smoke from the camp. Inside the concertina fence are military vehicles. James recognises the M1117 Guardian and the M1224 MaxxPro from his training. Suddenly, a rush of excitement floods his body and James fidgets and squirms in his seat. The reality and expanse of the endeavour are finally kicking in. Down below, snaking out from the gates of the yard, are two unarmed vehicles with trays, and from this distance, they look to be Ford Rangers. There is a whoop of joy from the soldier sitting next to James, and a 'fuck yeah' from the bloke opposite him. James can't help but smile.

The helicopter hums as it lowers closer to the grey earth, a tornado of dust rippling out from the shadow of the chopper. The men secure their harnesses and prepare for the descent from air to land.

This is it. This is what James has been waiting for.

CHAPTER 12

James—Misconduct—2014

Back in Australia, on Kaurna Country, while the rest of the battalion are sleeping in their barracks or on guard, Gunner James Bartelle is still awake, watching the shadows on the walls. The car headlights from the highway zoom and race across the walls, making elongated shards of yellowed light on the wallpaper. Since his deployment to Afghanistan, where he spent eight months mostly living underground and watching a computer screen, James is finding it increasingly difficult to sleep. He can feel his heart thumping and he knows his cortisol levels are too high for him to be able to relax enough to melt into dreamland—or nightmareland.

After the tour in Afghanistan, James and four of his comrades spent an exciting month travelling Europe in their civilian clothes. They'd earned their money and their autonomy, and now they relished the holiday and the freedom to party. Australian lads, full of confidence and pent-up energy, drank and smoked and danced and slept with pretty European girls. For James, it was his first trip overseas for pleasure, and the travel bug caught him firmly by both ankles. He loved the anonymity of being a traveller, as well as the way people stopped to ask him about his accent. James's height and blondish hair often drew attention. In bars—and there were plenty of bars—the boys were raucous and outlandish, often dominating the pool table and the jukebox. At the end of the month, having explored parts of Greece, Spain, and Turkey, the soldiers returned to Australia, to Adelaide, back to the Hampstead Barracks.

James struggled with the adjustment. The monotony of the routine, the lack of colour in the training yards, the shouting and demands of his superiors. James was reminded of his time in Afghanistan, the fateful helicopter drop, the memory of helping unload the bodies from the truck onto the dusty floor of the first aid hut. The smell of invisible blood surrounded him, infiltrating his senses, leaving a permanent scar. He remembered how each day as he crossed the dirt path between his sleeping quarters and the mess hall, his boots pressed into the crimson-stained dust—the dried blood of women and children—that was never washed away, because it never rained in the desert.

He couldn't seem to find any enjoyment in serving in the army now. Australia was pulling out of the conflict with the Taliban, despite the lack of infrastructure in place to ensure the safety of innocent civilians. But James didn't even care about that—not as much as he should. He couldn't see the point in worrying about what people in another country were doing. Fuck, he couldn't care what people in *this* country were doing to each other.

Staring at the shadows, he reaches for his collection of pills in their neat little white bottles. The army psych had been generous this week. Ignoring the recommended dose—*take one tablet at night*—James tips a handful of lightly coloured tablets into his shaking palm, tosses them into his mouth, and takes a long swig of vodka, which burns the back of his throat, but he doesn't give a shit.

He doesn't want his roommate to find him when it's all done, so James gathers the decency to leave the murky unit. Wandering along the path, a half-empty vodka bottle tucked safely between his jacket and his arm, James decides to venture past the small suburban brick dwellings and into the tree line, where twenty acres of woody land sprawls in the gloom. The sound of his footsteps is dulled by the moist compression of spongy grass and decaying leaves.

When James begins to feel the cloudy effect of the Valium and the Seroquel seeping into his bloodstream, he lowers himself down onto the cool, prickly grass and drinks from the bottle. He can feel his heart start to slow, his blood, turning thick octopus-ink black, coursing through his veins. James allows his thoughts to drift in and out as though he is surfing a wave. He wishes he was on his longboard now, dancing on the surface of the salty seawater. He longs to be held, buoyed by the safety of the board as frothy, phosphorescent waves roll underneath him. Instead, he is alone on the field of the quiet suburban army barracks, and no-one will know where he is until it is too late, and the thought makes him slightly nauseous yet relieved. James is ready to slow the pain, to leave the world with all its evil and darkness. James carries so much of the darkness inside of him, and he cannot live with the shame and the fear any longer. He takes another mouthful of vodka and lies down on the grass, clutching at the strands. He feels the tears sting his eyes and slowly, one by one, they roll down across his stubbly cheeks and land softly on the earth.

CHAPTER 13

Elle—Teaching—2014

She left Adrian back in 2010 after a dramatic night on the eve of her graduation from university. They had yet another argument and he yelled at her, "I hope you fucking die", and locked her out of the house. She slept in the car; well, she curled up in the driver's side and cried, listening to a Xavier Rudd song play on repeat. Elle had been drinking, so she could not exactly drive anywhere, and she was too ashamed to call any of her friends to come and get her. Confined like a prisoner to her silver hatchback, parked outside the sullen grey home where Adrian was throwing her belongings into a brown suitcase and cursing at the cat, she grieved.

The next day, after Adrian went to work, Elle used a broken brick to hurl at the bedroom window, smashing shards all over their king-sized bed. She kicked at the edges of broken glass and picked her way over the windowsill and into the house. Grabbing her suitcase, squeezing the cat into a carry cage, doing an anxious shit in the toilet and not flushing, Elle left Mayfield, left Adrian, and she did not look back. She silenced his calls and ignored his pleas to attend counselling together. Composing herself, Elle attended her graduation puffy-eyed and tired, but proud. After she collected her certificate and posed for photos in her gown and mortarboard, the roar of the crowd clapping filled Elle with gratification, and she allowed herself to feel pleased. Her mum was at the front of the audience, smiling broadly. Her dad sat up the back, arms crossed. Elle considered how hard she had fought to be where she was standing right now.

Afterwards, walking to the car, Elle turned to her parents, Simon three steps behind Pearl.

"I've left Adrian. Can I stay with you?" Her mum wrapped her long arms around Elle's shoulders, whispering in her ear, "Of course, my love. Whatever you need."

Her dad cuddled her next, in an awkward embrace, and he told her how proud he was.

"You are the first Bartelle to get a degree! Still counts, even if it is only a teaching degree," he said with a smirk.

The earlier sensation of gratification subsided and Elle tried to assert herself.

"Thanks, Dad. With honours, though." She smirked back at her dad, who was half-smiling with a creased forehead. Choked out a chuckle.

"Sure. Honours. Only eight people in your graduating class, though." He paused. And, as though an afterthought, he said, "Never mind. I'm proud of you, Eleanor." He rubbed her shoulder and said goodbye before walking away, bandy legs carving their way through the underground car park. Elle turned back to her mum and a look passed between them before Elle felt tears sting her eyes again.

* * *

Not long after hiding in the downstairs bedroom of Pearl's home for a few weeks, Elle received a call offering her a full-time job. Elated, she agreed right away. The following month, Elle began her teaching career on the sunny east coast of New South Wales.

She is happy being dramatic, exploring novels, and explaining poetry. She enjoys the energy of teaching and believes she is good at it. The routine suits her—early swim at the beach, drive to work, play-act with her drama classes, create with her English students, drive home. The initial terms of a teaching career do not hold the same jaded energy that comes after a decade of systematic issues, ridiculous pedagogical benchmarks, narcissistic leadership, lack of funding and resources, over-funding and mis-appropriation of capital, revamped and unrealistic disciplinary policies, and quite simply—teacher burnout. Luckily, Elle knows none of this yet. Blissfully on a professional trajectory, her past has nearly caught her, but for now, she is still withstanding the curling tendrils of the memories of the monster each time they reach for her.

Today, Elle is thirty-one years old and she is teaching a senior class when her phone vibrates in her pocket. She sneaks a glance. A number from Melbourne. She declines the call and continues her lesson on TS Eliot's poetry, explaining how the world ends—*whimpering*.

The students diligently copy down quotes and she annotates the language devices, oblivious to the boredom on the adolescents' faces. Elle is energetic and continues scribing the analysis, once again avoiding her feelings of dread and concern. Her ability to compartmentalise is quite the skill.

After the class had finished and while on playground duty at recess, she finally listens to the voicemail message that had been left. There is a formal yet hurried message from a "Ben"—*Lance Corporal Benjamin Laydon*. He sounds flustered yet firm. *"James has been involved in an incident. We are not sure of his whereabouts. We are concerned for his welfare and you are noted on his file as his next of kin. If he makes contact, please notify me on—"*

Elle feels the earth fall from around her. The concrete walls of A block suddenly tilt and sway. Her skin feels cold and the gaping hole in her stomach seems to fling open like an automatic door on an inner-city train, but she isn't on the same platform, and she is lurching, trying to find something to grab hold of.

After a few shallow breaths, Elle finds her feet and races up two flights of stairs and into the staff room, where she collapses onto a hard leather low-backed chair. A friend, a colleague, drops down beside her as she notices Elle's tears.

"Ez, are you okay?" she whispers, a wrinkled and sun-spotted hand wrapping around Elle's shoulders.

Elle takes a deep breath and tells her about the phone message. Tells the lady, between breath-catching sobs, "I can't reach James and I don't know if he is alive."

Elle feels sick again. She is so far from Adelaide and suddenly the distance between her and James is an abyss that she cannot cross.

"You need to go and tell the principal. You need to go home and be with your family," Her colleague offers empathetically. Elle inhales a whimper.

"No. Thanks, but that won't help. James is so far away, there is nothing I can do from here."

Elle stands up and smooths her skirt. She gathers herself, her computer, her worksheets, and her water bottle. She checks herself in the bathroom mirrors, tucks a strand of curly hair behind her ear and saunters back down to A block, where Miss Eleanor Bartelle cheerfully greets her class, the unruly and indisputably smelly Grade 9.

CHAPTER 14

James—Alive—2014

Much to his disdain, and another mistake to add to his growing list of shame, James does not die. He is found the next afternoon, groggy and incoherent, hungover as fuck. When his roommate noticed he was not in his room in the morning, he called the supervisor and said a little too much. He told Lance Corporal Laydon that Gunner James Bartelle had "been struggling for a while", and that "most nights he was high or drunk". Growling, Lance Corporal Laydon initiated a search and response team to locate the whereabouts of the soldier. Next of kin were notified—panicked, no doubt. But there were procedures that needed to be followed.

While the team searched each unit, checked each of the hangars, looked inside vehicles and checked security footage of the gates, Gunner James Bartelle was located by a soldier who was on a midday run on the eastern side of the barracks, having passed out from a concoction of substances. James was taken to the hospital where they offered him a psych evaluation. The thin and mousy psychologist asked him a series of questions that James found condescending.

"What are the thoughts, feelings, or behaviours that have been troubling you?"

In response, James lists the feelings of suicide, worthlessness, shame, and guilt.

"Has a particular event brought on these symptoms?" the psychologist asked.

With an eye roll and groan, James stated the obvious. "I'm in the fucking military." He scratched at the IV tube jutting out of the back of his hand.

Unperturbed, the lady scrawled some notes and continued.

"How long have you been feeling this way?" She met his eyes with piercing concern.

He could not hold her gaze, and he looked away before responding. "Since returning from tour."

The following weeks are a blur of meetings, appointments, and paperwork. After the "critical incident", Gunner James Bartelle is released back to his unit with a medical exemption and is issued a warning of misconduct. The misconduct report states that James was found intoxicated on Commonwealth property and that *a penalty may be instated pending further investigation*. James is pissed off at his roommate for telling Lance Corporal Layden that he had been using drugs and drinking on the nights he wasn't working. Without that knowledge, Layden wouldn't have slapped him with the mental health checks and the weekly mandatory testing.

The embarrassment runs deep through James. While he mostly stays in his unit, watching reruns of *Seinfeld*, James is conscious of his mates walking by, glancing in through the window or knocking to see how he is doing. Not wanting to talk about it, he laughs them away with a joke and a slap on the shoulder. Graciously, his mates don't press him for details. As they leave, James's smile fades away and he sits in the gloomy apartment, wondering how long the medical exemption to sever ties with the army will take. James knows he cannot stay here any longer or it will kill him.

James hates himself even more for failing yet again.

CHAPTER 15

Elle—Easter—2012

The start of the year has been a mixture of emotions. The stress of teaching is starting to affect Elle. With a range of students from diverse backgrounds, a dense curriculum, narcissistic leaders in the executive team, and the daily pressure of managing student conduct, Elle feels herself slipping into old patterns of behaviour. Each afternoon after work, around 5 pm, she reaches for the wine glass. *Just one,* she tells herself. Yet one glass often becomes three or four, as Elle sits on the verandah of her tree house and listens to the birds singing around her. In the distance, she catches glimmers of the lake shimmering in the dimming sunlight.

Elle's journal—she has always journalled—is filled with dreams, poems and charcoal sketches of her past. She outlines a prospective children's book using cartoon characters, where a young girl, Polly, is bullied by an ugly, big-headed character by the name of Loopus. Polly's purple cat, Rafferty, bravely rescues Polly from the shadowy clutches of bulbous-nosed Loopus. Scribbling away at the drawings, dabbing water paints on the insides of the pictures, Eleanor feels the frustration of the years of silence gnawing at her insides. It won't be long before the silence erupts and she begins to truly heal. For now, alone in her treehouse filled with dark memories of a coercive boyfriend, her real-life hero, Raff gently rubs his snout into her thigh, tail thumping, and he looks up at her with a dribbly smile of white teeth. Elle pats his tawny head and tells him, "Everything is okay".

The next morning, at the crack of dawn, Elle and Raff bound down the steep driveway and make their way towards the milky sand of the lake. Here, in the chill autumn air, they walk quickly along the edge of the water. Raff lunges ahead, chasing an unsuspecting seagull who was awoken from its resting place amongst the seaweed.

The sun—Bila—rises between the indigo lake and the olive-green mountain. Bila is wide and orange, piercing through the fog and mist, proudly arching her way above the water. Elle stands at the edge of the inland sea, watching the slow ascent of the sun. Deeply inhaling, Raff lying with his ears pricked at her feet, Eleanor reminds herself that today is a new day. Today is the first day of the rest of her life. The warmth of the morning rays kisses her cheeks.

It is a Tuesday and Elle needs to get home, shower, dress and prepare herself for the chaos of work. Her stomach churns at the thought of the lessons she needs to prepare, the parents she needs to contact, the pile of workbooks waiting to be marked. The calmness of the morning's energy in nature evaporates as her mind races through the upcoming jobs. But Elle is satisfied that Raff has had his walk and play, so now she can travel to school, content that he will sleep most of the day. Together they will run on the sand again this afternoon.

Back at her treehouse, she is listening to music while rolling through the morning routine. There is a break in the song, followed by an interruption of a *ding*.

A text message. From Bryce.

Have a great day.

Elle smiles widely and knows that the weekend cannot come soon enough.

The Easter long weekend is on the horizon. She will see Bryce on Good Friday, and then she will drive to her mum's place to spend time with the family. This is just what Elle needs to starve the demons for just a little longer.

CHAPTER 16

James—Easter—2012

It's Easter 2012. At first, James is incredibly anxious about the invitation, but after swallowing a few Valiums, he drives to his mum's place for the long weekend. Pearl dotes on her adult children, cooking, tidying, and laughing whenever the opportunity presents itself. Having received holidays from the army, James is in unwind mode. Elle is on school holidays and is visiting for the weekend. Everyone knows that James is great with his stories, telling yarns over a glass—or four—of wine at the large oval table in the middle of the dining room. He tells the story of the time when he was in Sydney with his mate from Brazil, Juan, and after a big night at Kings Cross, they were looking for a feed. The pair stumbled along the greying streets looking for something other than a 7-Eleven to be open. Juan was giggling, saying, "Zammez, back der, back der there waz a Pee-a-fach-ay." James tries to mimic his accent, but it comes out as a mixture of Italian and Thai. Never mind; he waves at the air in front of him, eyes sparkling, wine in hand. He continues the story.

"Pee-a-fach-ay?" he coos. "What the hell is a Pee-a-fach-ay?"

Juan grabbed him by the hand and said, "Come, I show you." Here, James stops and smiles broadly, taking his time with landing the punchline. He'd always had a flair for comic timing.

"So anyway, we cross the road and Juan pulls up short in front of a pie shop. Pie Face." Elle, Pearl, and James burst into laughter. "Pie Face! Pee-a-fach-ay!" They slap the table and laugh harder.

The next morning, James insists that he and Elle venture out for a surf. Elle has been keen to ride her longboard lately, and it gives James momentum to feel the vibe for the great Mother Blue again. He fondly remembers his time as a teenager, frothing over waves and riding his bodyboard before school, after school, and even sometimes instead of school. James senses in his muscle memory the deep connection he had felt to the ocean, the freedom and the power of the crashing waves beneath him. He remembers feeling small against some of the older surfers, his scrawny limbs floating atop an esky lid, resting in the shadows of those men with beards and dreadlocks. But he also remembers how he sat stoically on his board until it was his turn for a wave—albeit the smallest of the set—and slowly built his skills on the board. Over a few months, James earned a little shred of respect from the seasoned locals who rode shortboards, and the greying blokes who walked effortlessly across a longboard. Now in his mid-twenties, James feels a calling back to the great blue ocean and he longs for someone to enjoy the connection with him.

"Come on, sis!" James has loaded the boards on the roof and coaxes the dog into the back seat while waving to Elle as she walks out of Pearl's front door. Elle has cut her hair really short and James does not like it. Knowing the time to tell a chick how they should wear their hair is never right, James mostly keeps his thoughts to himself.

Now, they're coasting down the highway listening to Xavier Rudd. Raff is slobbering out the window and Elle is rolling a few smokes. James smiles and taps away at the steering wheel. The day is clear and crisp, and he is thankful for the wetsuits rolled in the back of his Subaru.

He turns off the highway towards Catherine Hill Bay, on Darkinjung Country, where the rugged coastline is sheltered by state forest and very little human development. Before hitting the old coal mining township of Catherine Hill, James turns left down a steep track that curls through the forest and opens to a run-down parking area on the outskirts of an abandoned mill. He parks next to the only other vehicle, a dilapidated white van with many stickers crowding the rear window. Looking around, James can see the green forest in front of him, the old mill behind, and the fresh blue sky filling all the space between. Raff bounds out of the car and marks his territory on every swaying casuarina and budding banksia. James unloads the surfboards while Elle squeezes into her wetsuit. They speculate about the conditions of the surf and weigh the pros and cons of taking wax with them. Leave the wax and take the towels, they decide mutually. While the sun is shining, the April wind is cool and they still have quite a walk ahead.

Picking their way over the timber bollards, passing the takeaway containers and crushed cans discarded by ungrateful visitors, Raff bounds ahead and the blonde siblings follow him. Ducking under low-hanging vines and weaving through the moaning trees on a rugged animal track, carefully avoiding too much damage to their boards, James and Elle finally find themselves exiting the forest and standing atop a jagged cliff face. At least twenty metres below is a crystal clear rockpool. They stand for a few moments, breathing in the salty air and looking for sharks circling the reef. The coast curls to the south. The sound of crashing waves echoes up the mountain.

Moving on, they tread lightly around the concave of the cliff and follow a grassy track down the hillside towards the swirling tendril of sand known as Ghosties Beach. At the bottom, they throw down their boards and sit for a few minutes while Raff pounces, pants, and paddles in the rock pools. There is still a way for the trio to walk, but the coastline is remarkable, untouched, and unforgiving. They are the only people here and, remarkably, James feels safe.

When they reach the break, dumping the towels, sunglasses, and car keys, James and Elle paddle their boards out together while Raff watches loyally from the place where he proudly guards the towels—what an important job he has. The water is clear enough to see the rocks below. The sets come in smoothly between four and five feet, a little bigger than Elle is keen for, so she stays a little closer to the shore and catches the shoulders of the broken waves. Yet James is captivated by the pulsating energy and he paddles directly into the swell, eager to let the water rush over his body and the moment of the wave below him to expand, sigh, crash, and reform. Each wave is unique, and he gives deep gratitude for the individual energy that surges and pulses in what he imagines are echoes. As he paddles onto each wave, James sacrifices himself, allowing the board to hold his weight atop the breaker until the sea changes her mind and shakes him free. After a short dance with the wave, he tumbles off the board and loses himself under the bubbles and pockets of sea-burst. For a moment, he hangs loosely and weightlessly below the surface, sound muffled in his ears with the water holding his body down. James is suspended in a watery space filled with peace and serenity. His thoughts are empty, and he is eternally grateful for the calm hands of the big blue nurturing his body. With a deep bubbling exhale, he surges up through the water and into the sapphire sky, snatching the leg rope to pull his board back into place. James straddles his board again, waiting for the next set. Looking across the water towards the shore, he sees the rugged cliff face etched into the land, with green foliage spreading like wings across the mountain. The land is untouched and undeveloped, and as he rests there, floating on the board, James thinks of the Darkinjung people. He wonders who lived here, feasting on the abundance of seafood and resting in the shelter of the Rainbow Caves during the middle of the day when the sun scorched the earth.

James wonders what it would be like to go back in time—back far enough in time that the only predator was the land itself.

CHAPTER 17

Elle—Thailand—Christmas, 2013

It is many years before Elle will receive a text from Lily about being stuck in Vietnam with her brother James, and well before Elle has given birth to Asher. It's late 2013. In a Messenger family group chat discussion, her cousin Stacey outlines all the perks of Christmas abroad, speckled with colourful emojis.

Cheap food
No-one has to cook/ clean up
Cheap accommodation
Beautiful weather
Cheap drinks
Resort-style living
No presents
Quality family time

The Bartelle and Whitlock families decide to venture to Thailand for Christmas. The last point, Elle thinks, subtly means, "Let's spend time with Auntie Leslie before she passes." Leslie is Pearl's youngest sister, who has had a life of pain and ill health. Meningitis ravaged her little body as a child and her heart never truly recovered. Now in her late fifties, Leslie walks slowly, her paper-thin skin stretching tight over a pained face. Walking the streets of Kata, Stacey, Mick, James, and Elle complain about how slow Leslie is. It's hot. The pavement is uneven. The streets are loud.

Eventually, the family sits down to an ocean-side meal prepared by a team of less-than-minimum-wage employees who keep their wine glasses filled and napkins fresh. The family share their Kris Kringle gifts, which, by Stacey's rules, must have been bought in Thailand. Auntie Janice opens hers first, revealing some embellished olive-green tablecloths. Next, Uncle Greg unwraps a stubbie cooler and a matching T-shirt that says *Chang Beer*. Then Pearl is thrilled with a pair of oversized fluorescent yellow sunglasses and a bamboo beach mat.

It's Elle's turn to open her present. James is ecstatic. He has already revealed he is her Secret Santa, which sort of defeats the purpose, but Elle doesn't mind. James has been drinking since 7 am and his eyes are dancing, his speech excited and buoyant. James continues to charm the crowd.

The gift is unwrapped and inside there is a poster tube. Elle unscrews the lid and slides out a rolled-up canvas. *Oohs* and *aahs* echo around the table. The sun blares down and the palm trees sway in the humid breath from the ocean. Elle unrolls the canvas and her eyes fill with tears. Happy tears.

She turns the artwork to show everyone, and there are gasps and chuckles of delight. Uncle Reg is slapping James on the back.

It's a beautiful charcoal sketch of James and Elle, heads tilted together, grinning. Elle recognises the photo the artwork is sketched from, taken at a Japanese restaurant in Adelaide after an Anzac Day parade. James was still in the army then, and Elle and her friend Katie had flown down for the celebration. When they arrived at the ceremony, James was already very drunk and the two-up games were quite expensive. Elle remembers how she told James she would buy all of his drinks. He was stoked by her generosity. Meaning well, she asked the bartender for straight raspberry soda instead of the double vodka and raspberry James had been drinking, just to sober him up a little. After a few drinks, the morning turned into late afternoon and three pubs later, James had wandered off and Elle and Katie found their way back to their rented apartment.

Around 10 pm, Elle was startled by her phone ringing. James wanted her to unlock the door to the apartment. Half-asleep, she fumbled with the latch and let him in. Behind him were two other people. A girl, about twenty-five, with heavy make-up and a thick waist. A guy, a bit older, with brown hair cropped short and wearing a plaid shirt. James introduced them as Maggie and Hugo. They talked loudly and went out onto the verandah to smoke. The laughter rippled like falling rocks throughout the tiny room. Katie was trying to sleep. Elle was trying to sleep. James and his mates did not seem to care. At some stage, in an exhausted daze, Elle joined them on the balcony and was shocked when James offered her a pipe. It was a glass pipe. And it was the second time in her life she had been offered a smoke of ice.

It really is a beautiful sketch, though. Elle is surprised James had thought of, and organised, such a personal and sentimental gift. After all, Elle considers, since being in Thailand, he's been using meth for six days straight now.

CHAPTER 18

James—Thailand—Christmas, 2015

Elle and James are sharing a room at the Centara Resort at Kata. He let his sister organise the accommodation, as she likes that sort of thing. The resort is sprawling, with two pools, a gymnasium and a grand hall where they can eat a three-course breakfast each morning. Well, one morning they did; the other mornings, James was hungover and not hungry. At this stage, nobody really knows about James's drug use. Well, Elle might have an idea but she has yet to say anything to him. Part of him is relieved and the other part is annoyed. He has been savvy at hiding the prescription pills and the meth. That shit is really fucking addictive. After his last bender in Adelaide, he told himself that was it. Although since being in Thailand for a few nights, James hears a prickly voice inside his mind whispering "addict" and "help". He silences the husky sound with another suck on the ice pipe chased with a swig of vodka.

James is still reeling from his first week in Phuket before his sister arrived. James flew in a week early and hit Bangla Road on the first afternoon. The bright lights, the loud music, the stench of septic water, barbequed street meat, and salty air wafted through the laneways. James befriended a random dude whose name now escapes him. The two young men skipped from bar to bar, drinking one-dollar beers and playing pool against the Thai bar girls. James switched from drinking beer to drinking vodka, vodka to rum, rum to smoking hash. Too soon, it was night-time and the tuk-tuk driver offered him some *ya ba*, which loosely translates to "crazy stuff" and is a mixture of meth and caffeine. James, aware of the death penalty in Thailand, aware of the thousands of people partying around him, aware of the hesitancy on his drinking buddy's face, smiled broadly, slapped the driver on the back and said, "Fuck yeah, take me!" For the next five days, James sprawled, danced, and smoked in a drug den on the outer streets of Patong.

The drugs were good. He floated between clouds in his mind and then surged with energy. He would dance and move his body, allowing all the pent-up anxiety to escape through his jagged movements. Smoking the *ya ba* through a gritty metal pipe, it tasted bitter and acidic. He washed it down with straight tequila. Here, in this calamitous room where bodies came and went, the electricity was disconnected, and the toilet was blocked and overflowing with shit, James did not have to think about the pressure of seeing his whole family for Christmas. He did not once think about making small talk and feeling judged. His social anxiety dissipated into the air like the smoke coming from his pipe.

When the money had been spent and the drugs were gone, James had the clarity to check his phone by tapping into wi-fi at a public bar. Sixteen messages from Elle. Shit. She'd been here for two days already. At first, James was annoyed that she was harassing him: *Where are you? I'm at the resort, thought you'd have checked in by now* … blah blah. But then he heard his stomach rumbling and remembered that the resort had room service. He grabbed his backpack and flagged a tuk-tuk back to Karon Centara Resort. Greeting him in the foyer, Elle was comforted to finally see her brother. James told her half the story about where he had been;

she believed him.

It is the evening after the Bartelles and Whitlocks' Christmas lunch. James survived the seaside banquet by guzzling mai tais and Long Island iced teas. He didn't have much of an appetite, but believed he ate just enough so no-one suspected he was high. During the present-giving—what were the chances of him drawing his sister as his Secret Santa receiver?—Elle was genuinely stoked with the portrait painting. Sure, it was James's idea and he had paid for the artwork two days ago, but he had to ask his cousin Stacey to pick it up from the gallery for him, as he was too inebriated to leave the resort room. Nevertheless, the gift-giving was not too tortuous, and James felt like he had won a few brownie points with his humour and chat. James was proud of himself for surviving another family gathering.

Afterwards, the family members hug and part ways, shuffling off to their various abodes, tummies filled with seafood, wine, and pudding. Some Bartelles and Whitlocks choose to have a nap. Some read a book while sipping on a coffee. James—well, James keeps drinking.

CHAPTER 19

Elle—Thailand Christmas Aftermath—2015

Elle is tired. The wine and the food have made her heavy and lethargic. She meets her cousins at a bar around 7 pm, stays for two drinks, and says goodnight. On her way out, she sees James and Mick have a tussle over the pool table. She hears shouting. She hears the name "Lance".

She sees James shrug Mick's hand from around his shoulder and storm outside.

"I'm going to go get arrested and spend the night in jail!" James shouts and staggers into the night. Elle tries to follow him, but he disappears in a sea of tourists down an alleyway lit with neon lights.

Mick and Elle debrief quickly.

"Let him go, Ez. He's gotta cool off."

Elle sighs and says goodnight again.

The tuk-tuk drops her off at the end of the laneway that snakes around to the grand entrance of the resort. She walks slowly, taking in the vibrant restaurants and street vendors along the way. People laughing and drinking and kissing. Kids running and chasing and tumbling. Thai vendors shouting and clapping and waving. Elle is exhausted by it all.

On the third floor, she opens her apartment door and inserts a plastic card into the slot, the lights illuminating the suite in a yellow hue. She notices her clothes first. Her eyes follow a trail of singlets, floral swimmers, aqua sarongs, and cargo shorts sprawling away from her suitcase like a microwave explosion.

Elle feels her blood run cold, pulling itself away from the surface of her skin and bracing for an attack. Her back pressed against the wall, she calls, "Hello? James?" But no-one answers.

Slowly, Elle inches towards the bathroom door, reaches around for the light switch, and turns it on, breathing a deep sigh when she sees it is empty. One more hiding spot to check: the space on the other side of her queen bed. Elle makes her way across the room and feels her heart jump from her chest. Empty space. Darkness. No moving shadows.

Now she has assessed that there is no immediate danger, Elle rushes to her suitcase. "What the actual fuck?" she hisses. Her clothes have been strewn across the floor and her passport and boarding passes tossed aside. Wait—they were in a zipped compartment in the inner lining of the suitcase, along with her extra cash. Looking, searching, scrambling, crying, Elle finds no money. It's all gone. Her last twelve thousand baht for the remainder of her holiday is missing.

In between her shock and fear, sadness surges, confusion, and finally, here—the anger. The rage.

That little fucker.

* * *

It's 3am when Elle hears James unlock the door. She sits upright in the darkness, having been too angry to actually fall asleep.

"What the fuck, James?"

"What?" He stumbles slightly and then collapses on his bed.

"My money, you prick. Where is my money?"

Silence. Then, "Oh, yeah. Shit," James starts. He closes his eyes and for a few beats, the room is closing in on them both. "Elle, it was fucked. These two guys, they were here, they said they were going to wait here until you got home and were going to *rape* you unless I gave them ten thousand baht!" His eyes are wide and now his hands are flapping. Elle feels her heart blacken even more.

"What do you mean, two guys were here? What two guys? How did they get here?" She is scared and confused and, yes, still very angry.

"I'm serious, Ez. They were Thai militia, I swear. I had to give them the money. They followed me here and I couldn't get them out. I had to. I'm sorry."

Head spinning, Elle rolls over and pulls the pillow over her face and sobs and sobs and sobs and sobs. Another memorable Christmas.

* * *

On the flight home, James is despondent, ashamed. He pulls his hood over his face and slouches against the window for the entire nine-hour flight back to Sydney. Pearl and Elle whisper next to him.

Help.

Rehab.

How?

Where?

Why?

Pearl is still confused.

CHAPTER 20

James—Thailand Christmas Aftermath—2015

After the long-haul flight followed by a two-hour train ride, while waiting for a taxi at the train station, James is slumped against a concrete wall at least ten metres from Pearl and Elle. He feels like shit. His head is thumping, his hands are shaking, and his throat is parched. Two solid weeks of meth and alcohol just to cope in the presence of his family. His rubber-band anxiety keeps pulling his chest tight, restricting then releasing, only to tug tighter again on the next breath. James rolls a cigarette and avoids the glaring eyes of passers-by, and those of his mum and sister. The thought of Pearl and Elle judging him sends his heart into another panic. James's dark cloud suffocates him further, pressing deep into his soul, and the shame surges. He knows that, if only he could find the words to articulate how he is feeling, maybe he could work through this with the support of his family. But the guilt and trauma and shame don't allow his voice to be vulnerable. Actually, he can't even truly recognise how he is feeling. He does not have the words to speak, even if he knows what to say.

Around the corner, a dishevelled man is calling out, "Hey! Hey, you! You gotta smoke, bro?" The man appears from around the concrete pillar and he is pushing a shopping trolley filled with plastic bags. He wears no shoes and the stench of stale beer follows him like a cloud. James doesn't say anything but rolls another smoke and hands it over. "Thanks."

James can see his sister watching the interaction. The homeless man wanders off through the crowd and towards the overpass of the train tracks and then glances back at James. James— dishevelled, empty eyes, overgrown fingernails, draped in black, still in his youth. James imagines he can see Elle's heart break and wishes the earth would open up and swallow him whole. He wishes he could step in front of a moving train. He wishes he could hang himself with his belt right here, right now, at this fucking train station. Then they would all have something to watch.

* * *

James never apologises for stealing from his sister. He couldn't find the words. The shame was too great. After returning from their trip, Pearl tells him how she transferred the stolen money to his sister so that Elle could continue her summer holiday at Byron Bay with her girlfriends. Because "you know, she deserves a good holiday".

CHAPTER 21

James—Acknowledgement—2014

It is Friday, 30 May 2014, and James has an appointment with Dr Wilson. James sits in the waiting room, bulky, filling the small space of lime-green walls, two plush La-Z-Boys, and drawn venetian blinds dangling behind him. James sits on one of the navy chairs, scratching at his blistered hands. His foot is nervously tapping the lino. The *SF* on his baseball cap stands for the San Francisco Giants, and his black-and-orange sneakers match the cap. Since his trip to America, James has been beginning to think more about his ancestral roots, and he is longing to return to Cali for a much longer time. Rent an apartment in Santa Cruz or even San Diego and surf all day, drink Iron Springs and fernet by evening. James imagines how the girls will swoon at his accent and how he will join a CrossFit gym and rip his body to shreds. One day, he thinks, he will walk the Appalachian Trail just like Bill Bryson in *A Walk in the Woods*. His thoughts are racing across the ocean when he hears his name being called.

"James?"

It's a half-statement, half-question. Of course it must be James—no-one else is crammed into this room.

"Um, yep." James rubs his thighs and stands up, not knowing if he should offer a hand to shake or light up a cigarette to calm the shakes he is starting to lose control of. The room suddenly feels even smaller than it is, and the doorway is swaying. Dr Wilson smiles at him and steps aside, widening the passageway and lessening the immediate threat James is feeling. Over the past six years, Dr Wilson has worked with many ex-soldiers and knows how to recognise trigger points.

"Nice hat, James," she says with a smile and a nod.

Unknowingly to James, Dr Wilson has focused his attention away from the threat of claustrophobia. James returns the gesture of a smile and feels his breath escape in a long, slow exhale. The room stops swaying as he thinks about the colours of the SF logo. He taps his head twice and walks into the consultation room. James will later learn this valuable strategy to avoid the onset of a panic attack—refocusing on something tangible. Yet, for now, he merely appreciates the warmth of Dr Wilson's energy.

Inside the consultation room, James gravitates towards the large green lounge stretching out underneath a window where, across the tops of tomb-like buildings, James can see crowns of skyscrapers and, somewhere, a glint of blue water. He sits down and takes off his cap, cradling it like a small child in his arms. He fingers the logo to stop his hands from shaking.

"You've had quite a journey, James," Dr Wilson states matter-of-factly.

"Um, yep, that's true." James scans the room and is grateful the door has been left open. He can see the waiting room; no-one is there. He accepts a glass of water that Dr Wilson has put in front of him.

"Should I start from the beginning?" he asks.

"Let's."

* * *

Dr Wilson scrawls in her notepad, and later that night she sits at her desk, by lamplight, and types her report to send to DVA.

Attention Doctor Satvi,

Please continue the care of this member who has recently been discharged from the Australia Regular Army (ARA), where he worked as an Air Defender for around 5 years.

Mental State Examination:
He was pleasant and cooperative during the examination and was able to provide adequate information about his personal and professional history. He seemed obviously withdrawn and anxious, particularly when enquired about his childhood.

While he served in the army, James was seeing the army doctor with whom he claims he had a good rapport. He generally remained quite well during his service, however, has been diagnosed with a number of conditions this year including panic disorder, social phobia, and alcohol abuse. His symptoms include becoming agitated in crowded places, avoiding any social interactions, being worried about his future and suffering flashbacks of his past traumatic experiences. He has tried to overcome these symptoms by drinking alcohol and taking illicit drugs.

James was involved in an incident whilst serving in the army whereby he required a left shoulder arthroscopy with labral repair and recovered well from this.

On his separation health examination today he has some ongoing health issues that require follow-up. There is a history of childhood sexual abuse and he has been seeing counsellors through WCS. His recent psychiatrist review, due to a deterioration in his mental health, diagnosed him with reactive depression. It is unclear whether this condition is deep-seated or reactive due to his history of abuse and recent counselling intervention. He has commenced Escitalopram 10 mg and is tolerating this well. He was also taking Seroquel 25 mg nocte to assist with sleep and severe agitation, which appears to have settled.

Member is currently unfit for operational deployment but he can be rehabilitated from a medical viewpoint.

Primary Duties
2-14 Unfit for shift work
2-18 Not to work in stressful environments
2-20 Not to work more than 40 hours per week

General Service Duties
3-8 Unfit to drive ADF vehicles
3-17 No access to live ammunition

Health Care Requirements
4-1 Access to pharmaceutical resupply
4-3 Access to specialist health support
7-2 Under active medical treatment

Doctor Wilson finishes her report and emails her findings to the Department of Veterans Affairs, shaping the course of James's life.

Now he is unemployed and unemployable.

Now he will be on a pension.

Now he has a label.

Now he will rely on pharmaceuticals to steady his mind.

CHAPTER 22

Elle—Recovery—2014

James is medically discharged from the army and he comes to stay with Ellie in her tree house tucked into a rainforest. It is a leafy suburb on the outskirts of Pacific Palms on Worimi Country, notorious among surfers and artists alike. A few years ago, Elle bought the home with the second of her terrible partners, this man worse than the first one she married. Like a cliche, Elle accepted the love she thought she deserved—which was not much—and this did not end well. After Adrian, Elle had started her career and rented a tiny two-bedroom apartment by the seaside. Loneliness soon took hold and Elle went searching to fill the void in her life, first with wine, then with men, and usually both together.

Ethan was tall, brown-skinned, with cornflower-blue eyes and a collection of facial piercings. First, the sexual attraction was instant. Next, Elle was attracted to the way this man hated society. His strong opinions about politics and social justice intrigued her. She loved the way he surfed, skated, and used graffiti as a way of sticking it to "the man". Elle, still mostly a rule-follower, enjoyed living on the edge with Ethan. She was swept up by his unending lust and the way he seemingly idolised her by showering her with gifts, affection, and words of affirmation.

Ethan always had cash, crisp yellow and green notes, and he was willing to spend it on her. Strangely, once Elle saw him writing tiny inscriptions on a faded piece of paper. When she asked what it was, he said, darkly, that he kept a list of names of people who owed him something. Then, turning away from her, he folded up the tiny piece of paper and tucked it into a crevice in his wallet. Elle's curiosity was one of her many downfalls, but she was not cautious enough to avoid the clutches of this criminal.

Soon, Elle and Ethan were buying a house together. She had a steady income; he had the deposit, but a minimum-wage job. Elle should have asked more questions about why he always had cash, but instead, she allowed herself to be ricocheted into another volatile and passion-filled romance and they decided to buy the tree house at Smiths Lake. Ethan continued to work in Newcastle and would visit on the weekends. Each weekend was filled with drugs and drink, surfing and sex. Soon, though, Elle started to see the anger in Ethan, his controlling nature and his inability to go a few hours without smoking a cone. The first time he screamed at her, he called her a "stuck-up cunt". The second time he screamed at her—*"fucking selfish cunt"*—he also punched the wall next to her head, making her scream and cower. From there, it seemed that every conversation ended with him bellowing at her.

After a whole tumultuous year of trying to leave him (but he would always apologise, buy her gifts, or else threaten suicide if she did not take him back), Elle's mental health was at an all-time low. She had acknowledged the trauma from her childhood and she recognised the abusive cycle she was trapped in with Ethan, but she had isolated herself from her mum and her friends. She was worlds away from her other, calmer life. Elle frequently had "black days", as she referred to them, where she would lie in bed with the covers over her head and cry. Ethan would rub her back and tell her she "needed to choose a good time over feeling shit". After his never-ending persistence, she would accept a swig of vodka and that black day would roll into night.

As low as Elle felt, however, she could not leave Ethan until her life was nearly taken from her. The miserable relationship finally ended when he attempted to suffocate her with a pillow and kept her kidnapped in the back of his van for eight hours, torturing her.

Rewinding, the couple had decided to go to a bush rave out the back of Cessnock, in a remote part of the state forest. Elle had not been to something like this before, and part of her was excited. The party was crowded with people dressed in fringed crocheted tops, leather miniskirts, tie-dyed shirts, and baggy fisherman pants. There was a large stage surrounded by fairy lights, and inflatable mushrooms hung from the trees. Scattered throughout the dance floor were fire pits producing circling smoke and illuminating the people dancing, gyrating, puffing. Being passed around were tabs of acid and bottles of pills, which Elle did not accept. She was watching with a strange sense of awe as the festivalgoers let down their dreadlocked hair, partying through the night. Ethan was in his element. By midnight, Elle was tired, and she made her way back to Ethan's van, which was nestled on the outskirts of the clearing but not quite far enough away for her to not hear the chest-pounding beats of the electronic music all night long.

When the sun raised her smouldering head above the cracks of the gum trees, Elle was keen to pack up the campsite and make a move home. Ethan was nowhere in sight. She had to work the next day and was already thinking about the preparation she needed to do before class, feeling agitated. Wandering over to the festival, searching for Ethan, Elle was surprised at how many people were still awake, grooving haphazardly in the misty clearing. Eventually, Elle found Ethan talking with a girl who was only wearing a black skirt, her thin boobs drooping down her rib cage. Elle wanted to seem cool and accepting of this chick's display of sexual freedom, so she hugged the girl like they were long-lost friends.

They embraced and giggled like schoolgirls. Elle stole a glance at Ethan, who seemed pleased with Elle's demeanour. A wave of relief circled her body. After some incoherent chat with the thin-boobed girl whose pupils were like black holes, Elle took the opportunity to tell Ethan they should get going.

"I'm not ready." He glared at her.

"Okay, I'll go and pack up the van and I'll pick you up in about an hour." Elle waved goodbye and picked her way between the foliage and rubbish on her way back to the vehicle.

An hour later, there were still about twenty people scattered around the clearing in various states of coming down and waking up. Driving the aubergine VW to the outskirts of the stage, Elle waited with the car idling in neutral for Ethan to come over. And he did. In a rage. He got into the passenger side and loomed over her. Her hands gripping the steering wheel, Elle was terrified.

"What the *fuck* are you doing?" he roared at her. "Drive the fucking car."

Shaking, Elle started to roll the car away from the dusty remnants of the dying party, found the gravel track and plunged down the bumpy hill.

In her recurring nightmares, she remembers the white spit at the side of his mouth. She remembers the acrid smell of his breath. She remembers the abrupt stopping of the van, its tyres skidding, when he yanked on the handbrake and painfully grabbed her wrists. She remembers his words and his venomous tone for many years to come.

"You are a selfish cunt. I'm going to kill you and bury you out here in the forest where no-one will find you." Elle's blood ran cold with fear. Suddenly snatching her, he manhandled her into the back of the van, took the phone, and locked the doors. She was crying, spluttering words of confusion, attempting to placate him, trying words of affection and reassurance. She exhausted herself begging and pleading for him to let her out of the van alive. *Please, let me out alive.*

The ex-lovers landed in court, and Ethan was charged with six counts of assault and intimidation with a weapon. Whilst Elle was relieved the relationship was finally over, the horror of that night, trapped in the van in a remote state forest, would never leave her.

Many times her heart will stop beating when she thinks she sees Ethan from a distance, his bald head bobbing through crowds, or the sight of a maroon van decorated with stickers. Years later, when COVID strikes in 2020 and masks are mandated, her intense anxiety will return, crippled with panic when she tries to wear a face mask. She is triggered back into a state of fear and terror, remembering the pillow held tightly over her face, unable to breathe freely. Her doctor will write a letter of exemption, but everywhere Elle goes, she is judged and challenged for defying "health advice".

"You need to have a mask on to be here"; "Why can't you just put on a mask?"; "I can't serve you without a mask."

Even seeing people wearing masks makes it difficult for Elle to breathe. But for now, in 2014, she lives peacefully as a single woman in the tree house with her dog, Raff. Raff is a long-legged ridgeback cross who has a loud bark and is very protective and loyal. Finally, Elle has a love that is unconditional and non-transactional. She fell in love with Raff's big brown eyes and kangaroo tail at the Wyong Pound; she made a promise that they would spend every weekend together, no matter what. Now Raff gives her an excuse each morning to bound out of bed and together they skirt the edge of the lake in the rising of the sun. They watch the colours of the sky turn from navy blue to hibiscus purple to baby blue. Elle throws a stick to Raff and he leaps out across the shallow water, smiling, his fur rippling with joy. Sometimes they visit Cellito Beach at dawn, where they are the only souls walking the beach.

Elle looks across at the headland of littoral rainforest and imagines the Worimi people living their lives there, fishing the seas and hunting the lands, loving Country and keepers of Mother Earth. The Worimi people would have seen exactly what Elle sees now, as Cellito Beach has yet to be touched by the inky stain of White greed and insidious development. The beach is so pristine that often Elle swims naked in the turquoise water, washing away years of anger, fear, and resentment. It is during this time in her life that Elle is truly happy. She invests much time into her self-worth, her mental health, her goals and dreams. Elle sheds the anxiety that has held her back, unfurls her wings, and sets herself free of the heavy weight of an ugly man's hands around her throat, under her skirt. She is single and unbound.

Living alone, Elle chooses not to have a television connected. Instead of mindlessly watching, she spends hours listening to music, sketching with charcoal and writing in her journal. Lying on the spongy couch on the verandah, Elle smokes cigarettes and writes poetry, languid letters exposing her thoughts, fears, and dreams. Later, she ventures down the steps to the first floor where, in what used to be an office, she has converted into a yoga space. The room sits in the corner of the house. When stretching on her yoga mat, Elle can look through a glass sliding door where all she sees are waving palm trees and dancing, colourful birds. She loves this space, sprawling and breathing and spending more time in lion pose than any other.

Elle is reclaiming her identity. First Lance, then Adrian, and more recently Ethan, these men in her life have stolen from her and she is outraged. Yet yoga and meditation calm her anxiety, balance her emotions and keep her fear at bay.

Elle is working as a teacher and she drives thirty minutes to her school. Along the way she listens to audiobooks such as *The Happiness Project*, *The Happiness Trap*, and *Wherever You Go,*

There You Are. Listening to the insightful words of wisdom—*what a childish pleasure to have someone else read aloud to me*—Elle nods in agreement and tries to remember quotes to scribble in her journal later.

She escaped the night of terror by stealing the keys to the van after Ethan got out to take a piss. He had been smoking a lot of pot and mumbling about how sick he was and how the acid trips had made him act out. His rants oscillated between wanting to stab her with scissors and then kill himself, like Romeo and Juliet, to crying and saying how sorry he was, that it was the drugs that were making him do this. He said he could not let her go now, because she would leave him.

Grabbing the keys, she locked the doors, shaking and crying, and reversed the van into his leg. In the rearview mirror, she saw Ethan fall down in surprise and jump up again, running with his fist flailing. Blurry-eyed and hyperventilating, the drive to town was hazy. Eventually, Elle was able to pull over and locate her phone, which Ethan had hidden, and between throaty gasps, she called a friend to come and get her. She told her friend how Ethan had a knife and wanted to kill her and bury her in the mountains. The friend told her to stay where she was and to not move. The next thing Elle remembered was the police vehicles arriving and then someone wrapping her in a blanket and driving her to the station.

Next, the principal was notified, as it was Monday and Eleanor should have been at work; if only she hadn't been kept captive all night. After hearing what had happened, and with a grandmotherly nature, the principal contacted the school counsellor and Elle was swaddled with support while she tried to process the events of the past twenty-four hours; the past two years; the past *centuries* of patriarchal abuse and intergenerational trauma. In a tiny drop in the ocean of time, Elle spent two weeks sleeping in a safe house. The police had not yet located Ethan and chances were he was plotting his revenge. Statistics prove that the man's revenge would be bloodier than the first attack. But this beachside shack was just what Elle needed. Mostly, she was able to sleep in peace, but the nightmares still came. Flashes of Ethan's white teeth, the blade of the knife, the pressure of his hands on her legs. Waking in a pool of sweat, she would light a cigarette and reassure herself she was safe.

Before work, Elle rode her longboard between the rocks, sailing on the waves and freeing her broken soul. After two weeks had passed, and the police had arrested Ethan, issued him with the apprehended violence order, and Ethan's mother had emptied the tree house of his possessions, Elle was ready to return to her home by the lake. It was nerve-racking being in that space again. The first thing she did was rip the bedding from the queen-sized bed and burn the doona cover in the backyard fire pit. Then she bought a bright red floral cover and crisp white sheets. Next, she bought some flame-red paint and created a feature wall in her bedroom. There was something about the colour red that was powerfully soothing for Elle. She adorned the wall with quotes, photos, drawings she had made of fairies, and pencil sketches of animals and ocean waves. The corner was her happiness wall. She even made a collage of every sunrise photo she had ever taken. Hanging the collage on the bathroom wall, every time Elle looked at it, she would remember Xavier Rudd's lyrics to his song "Follow the Sun" and the gentle reminder that each day is a new day and to always cherish this breath.

Slowly, intentionally, Elle reclaimed her home, her body, her mind.

* * *

James comes to stay with Elle. Together they are sober, but they enjoy rolling and smoking tobacco and sipping instant coffee.

James hides the pills from his sister—which he finds easy after all the practice he has had. They laugh as they tow a canoe down to the lake's edge. Raff excitedly bounds along ahead. They paddle out into the lake, pull up on a milky sandbank, and cast a fishing rod into the deep green channel. With little attention to the line, James decides to wander along the sand, sinking slightly in the mudflats. He watches the yellow canoe bob silently in the current. Elle casts the line again. James feels the setting sun on his face and smells the salty, inky seaweed swaying and drying in clumps littered around his feet.

He will stay for ten days. Alcohol-free for ten days. The siblings will surf and fish and watch *Breaking Bad* from start to finish. They will laugh and banter, smoke and snack. James loves the simplicity of Elle's life. He thinks about how similar, yet different, they are. The same beginning to their story, with a very different middle, and an uncertain ending. The forks in the family tree twist, curve, and wind their way through the forest of this life they share.

CHAPTER 23

Elle—Losing a Loved One—2015

Auntie Leslie has become sicker and sicker. The doctors say her kidneys are not working well and her heart—the one that has the mechanical tick—is also struggling.

Elle has many fond memories of her Auntie Leslie. Early imprints from when the young aunt came to stay with Pearl and Simon when the children were small, Elle maybe seven years old. Auntie Leslie was beautiful and fun, loving and warm. She was always present at birthday parties and family gatherings. In years to come, Elle will deeply miss the way her aunt always took control of parties—diligently assigning who would bring which food and what time the cake would be cut.

Back in the early 2000s, when Elle returned from her travels through San Francisco and London, it was Auntie Leslie who suggested she stay in the spare room at the back of her fibro home in the beachside suburb of Umina, on Guringai Country. The home was small and dark inside, yet each wall was adorned with shelves of knick-knacks including porcelain dolls and blown-glass vases. Auntie Leslie had many framed photos that hung haphazardly across the walls and lent precariously atop wooden bureaus. Elle remembers running her fingers across the smiling faces of her deceased grandmother and the squinting eyes of the tribe of Whitlock siblings posing together beside an old car circa the 1960s. Elle recognised her mother. Pearl, the eldest of the six siblings, was a tall wavy brunette wearing a faded red shirt and an oversized T-shirt that hung off one shoulder. In the photos, Leslie—probably aged ten—clutched her older sister's hand and looked up at her with a crooked smile and one dimple on her cheek. Elle liked looking at these photos—glimpses into carefree moments of the past.

It was Aunt Leslie who encouraged Elle to enrol in university—which she did—and gave Elle a job at the car spares shop Leslie owned with her husband, Reg. Once a week after work, Leslie would take Elle to the local pub, where they would drink a middy of light beer mixed with lemonade. It would be soon afterwards that Elle would start working at this particular venue, thanks to Leslie's familiarity with the staff. Social and friendly, Leslie had an easy way of making people love her. Elle remembers fondly that Leslie was mostly well during this time of living together.

Yet today, Leslie's aging body is giving up. In the weeks leading up to this day, Elle has made many day trips to the hospital and sat next to her tired aunt and held Uncle Reg's hand. It was a Thursday night when Elle stayed with Reg because she could sense his fear and sadness. After all, Leslie and Reg had been high-school sweethearts. Now in their sixties, the decades together have left deep imprints. Reg and Leslie do not have children of their own, and Elle likes to think of them as her second parents. On this particular Thursday night, Reg and Elle go out for dinner, Elle ordering the spare ribs and Reg ordering the caesar salad. They giggle when the waitress serves the plates of food incorrectly. Reg is too consumed with worry for his beloved wife to eat much, and Elle is ravenous after not eating much at all during the day. They make small talk about the venue, the food, and the weather. It's Reg who brings up Lance.

"Lance called me the other night." He swallows a piece of lettuce. Sips his beer.

"Oh, yeah?" Elle raises her eyebrows. Wipes her chin with the napkin.

"He said you are going through some stuff. And that James is using drugs. Is that true?" Reg looks directly at her.

Elle bristles at his judgemental tone and asks, "Did Lance say *why* James is using drugs?" Placing her knife and fork on her plate, she folds her hands under her chin and leans towards her uncle, searching for any hint of knowing.

Behind thick glasses, Reg looks away from his niece.

"Look, Lance seemed genuinely upset that you haven't returned any of his calls lately. He thinks you're depressed."

Depressed … Ha! thinks Elle. She scoffs aloud and Reg startles.

"I'll tell you why I haven't spoken to him. *And* I'll tell you why James is using drugs. But you won't like what you hear." Elle surprises herself with her own confidence and conviction. Maybe it's the wine. Right now, she does not feel ashamed of what Lance did to her, but rather, she feels a burning desire to crush Lance's popularity and expose his true darkness.

For the next eight minutes, Elle speaks clearly and concisely. She tells her uncle Reg what she could never tell him when she was a child.

Afterwards, Reg puts his head in his hands, shaking from side to side. Eventually, he raises his head, looking older than before. He takes Elle's hands in his, tears glistening in his eyes.

"I'm sorry."

"Don't be sorry, Uncle Reg. Be mad. Be mad that Lance is *still* telling lies." She swallows the remainder of her wine and detects a lightness to her mood. The burden has been shared, and it is easier to hold. An afterthought catches her off guard and the flutters in her chest return.

"Uncle Reg, please don't tell Auntie Leslie. It will crush her." Elle scorns herself for fleetingly thinking she is glad Leslie is in a coma.

The rest of the evening swims by in uncomfortable silence.

* * *

Today, the doctors have inadvertently suggested that the concoction of medications that Leslie has been taking for the past twenty years has ruined her kidneys. There were the pills she needed for her heart, which raised her blood pressure, so there were more pills for that. Her cholesterol was too high, so Leslie was prescribed another box of medications. Soon, Leslie had a whole meal of tablets to take each day. A few years prior, she had heart surgery and afterwards, her body reacted to the antibiotics, sending her into a two-week coma. The antibiotics did not work, and the doctors gave her medications newly on the market. As was the triumphant case with the Whitlock genes, Leslie put up a fight and recovered from the infection, even surprising the doctors with her recovery.

Now, years later, her organs are struggling and there is little left the doctors can do to help her.

Pearl, Eleanor, and Reg sit sullenly around the hospital bed. Lights blink and the monitor beeps. People wearing coats come and go, carefully picking their way between the visitors, politely nodding and offering weak smiles of understanding. At 3 pm, Leslie is taken off the last of the medication that has kept her heart ticking. She is asleep, with only a tube helping her to breathe. Raspy noises escape from her parched throat. Glucose is pumped into a thin blue vein in her wrist through a small tube; the last of the human intervention.

Silently, Pearl brushes her sister's hair, smears lip balm on her cracked and swollen lips, and whispers to her. Elle holds her aunt's papery hand and squeezes her cold fingertips. Reg wipes at tears rolling down his cheeks.

At 10:34 pm, Leslie takes her last breath.

Elle has never seen a dead person before. She is surprised by how grey and old her aunt looks, lying there under a white sheet, mouth agape. In the nights to come, Leslie's ghastly face and gaping, toothless mouth will wake Elle in the middle of the night. Yet in the months following, Elle will remind herself of all the other memories she shared with her aunt. The tanned, plump face with sparkling eyes and a busyness about her hands, squeezing Elle in for a cuddle. She will look at all of the photos of better times together: blowing out the candles atop a chocolate cake with strawberries, smiling at the camera from underneath a cap while fishing in a tin boat, Leslie's arm wrapped around small Elle's shoulders, wearing matching yellow and blue netball uniforms on a sunny day. These are the faces of her aunt that Elle chooses to remember.

The day of the funeral has arrived. The extended family and abundance of friends of the late Leslie Whitlock fill the car park of the leafy, English-styled gardens of the cemetery. Elle stands with her cousin Stacey and together they share small talk about the weather, nervously crossing and uncrossing their arms. People mill around the entryway, waiting for the signal to enter the auditorium. Familiar and unfamiliar faces look at Elle. Someone taps her on the shoulder and pulls her in for a sympathetic embrace while dabbing at the corners of their eyes.

Entering the auditorium, the family fills not only the first two reserved rows of wooden bench seats, but they crowd into the first four. Elle sits between her mother and Stacey, and they all hold hands. Mick sits in front, intently watching the priest take his place behind the lectern. A song by Simon and Garfunkel plays through the speakers as a slideshow of photos light up the room. Elle sniffs back her tears.

The service begins and soft words are spoken. Pearl delivers the eulogy, bravely choking back her tears. Next, Stacey, Leslie's eldest niece, takes the stage and recites a poem about memories and a garden of flowers. Elle wipes her eyes as she listens. Clutching a piece of paper in her shaking hands, it is Elle's turn next to read a short psalm in loving memory of her beloved aunt. Crossing the stage, she looks out at the sea of faces. Searching. She scans the back of the room in case he is skulking on the edges of the crowd. He is not here. Elle lets out a relieved sigh, collects her breath, and speaks with as much clarity as she can muster.

Afterwards, at the wake, people will hug her and say how well she spoke. Through tears, Elle will politely say thank you. Distantly thinking of her brothers.

One brother is in rehab. The other brother uninvited. A mixture of anger and sadness engulfs her.

CHAPTER 24

Elle—Summer Holidays—2012

It is December 2012. The hot, steamy humidity cloaks the Central Coast and James, Elle, and their two cousins are staying at Pearl's place. The house sits on a wide, grey lake where black swans sit idly among the abandoned trolleys and floating discarded McDonald's cups. But the house is beautiful. It sits proudly on the parade, a two-storeyed bright yellow abode. Inside, everything is white and fresh and crisp. With her age, Pearl has become wary of germs of all types, using her homemade remedies and potions to deter, discourage, and terminate little bugs and pests. There are no pests this December, save the mosquitoes who fly in from the mudflats of the lake. Downstairs, the kitchen opens invitingly into the living room. A large corner couch frames the room and Elle's amateur art frames the walls, glowering down with an obscure sexual stare.

The drooping pine tree blinks its fairy lights in the corner of the room. The house smells of pine and cinnamon and wine. The outside lights are bright and there is laughter heaving from the small deck.

Elle, James, Pearl, Mick, and Stacey are playing a board game around the glass table. The young ones flick ash from their cigarettes and take swigs from their glasses. Pearl laughs openly and sips her green tea, buoyed by the company of her children and her niece and nephew. Pearl remembers when Stacey was only six months old and her brother, Reg, dropped Stacey off to stay with her. Pearl hadn't had children of her own then, and she smothered that sweet-smelling, chubby little baby like she had loved her own five siblings. Pearl knew she wanted a tribe of children; she just hadn't met the right man.

Mick and Stacey had arrived from Melbourne two days earlier and brought laughter and ease to their cousins. Elle and James are close to the southern family, more so than the cousins who live just around the corner. Mick and Stacey ooze sarcasm and the casual, laid-back attitude that comes with being born with the Whitlock genes.

"What do you call a deer with no eyes?" crows Mick.

"No fucking idea!" shouts James.

The family roars with laughter. The lights bear down. The heat simmers. Christmas is here.

The next night the fam decided to walk up to the local hotel. Other uncles and cousins meet there, and they share a meal of T-bone with mushroom gravy, or chicken parmy with chips and salad. The Whitlocks take up twelve seats, the longest table and by far the loudest.

It is after dinner and the young cousins go to the pool room. Here they sink schooners and pool balls, laugh crudely, and recall family memories.

"Remember when you guys lived in Ettalong and you had that dog … Sasha … yeah, that German shepherd?" cousin Sarah asks Mick.

"Remember when we went hiking through the national park but didn't have any food? We had to creep down to that stranger's house and tried to sneak down the driveway but she caught us and we were so scared of getting busted!" cooed Elle.

"Yeah, remember when Lance chased us through the bush that time?" Mick laughed.

Elle feels the familiar floor-falling-from-under-her feeling. The swaying and trying to grab hold of something tangible and real. Her breath catches somewhere between her belly button and her throat.

She forces a smile. Her mascara is smudged.

"Yeah, I remember," Elle responds. "What about the time Lance put the bucket on my head at his thirtieth birthday party and whacked me over the head and filmed it? He shared it with everyone." She is speaking louder and her voice is shrill. "I was so drunk and disorientated. What about that? What a fucking dick." Elle takes another long swallow of her vodka and tonic. Her rowdy and drunk cousins hush a little, steal an awkward glance between each other, and then look away.

Her words have changed the mood. A few minutes ago they were all laughing and sharing stories. Now Elle feels angry and confused. Her cousins and her brother sense the energy shift. Elle glares at Mick, waiting for him to say something. He looks away. She turns to Stacey, waiting, expecting. Nobody looks at her. The heaviness in the room is crushing. The firmness on her chest is like a man's hand holding her down. *Say something!* They avoid her eyes. They don't ask any questions.

Elle can't stand it anymore. The crushing silence. The awkward avoidance. The elephant stomps through the room. It chases her.

She grabs her bag and leaves the pub through the exit glowing to her right. Her lungs fill with warm and sticky air as she slumps down into the gutter, in the shadows of the passing cars. She lights a smoke and inhales her deep, deep frustration.

Three puffs in, she hears the swinging doors of the hotel open and close behind her.

James.

He sits down next to her, smoke in hand. They watch the traffic passing, hear the roar of laughter from inside the tavern. James playfully nudges her with his elbow and says, "Hey, sis."

Elle rests her head on his shoulder and blinks back her tears.

"Hey, Ez; he's an arsehole," James says. His eyes twinkle and there is a smile etched into his bearded face.

Elle nods. Sniffs. Drags her smoke. Exhales loudly.

"I know what he did, Ez. I know why you hate him so much." James speaks soberly and seriously now. His body is tense.

Elle holds still. Did she hear him correctly? Did James see what happened? Did James, a little seven-year-old boy, open the door under the stairs one day after hearing movement behind the hot water system? Elle freezes, worried about the fallout, the shame, the outrage. Her blood runs cold and, again, her world tilts on its axis, ready to throw her off course, out into the street, in front of a moving bus. *Tick. Tick. Tick.* Time slows; her breathing stops.

"I know … I know, because he did it to me, too." And James squeezes Elle so tightly she isn't able to fall away or sink into the darkest depths of the pain. She inhales sharply and deeply, feeling the rush of warm air fill her lungs. She still has two feet on the ground. Elle's world has not ended—that is soon to follow. At this moment, hearing James confess a truth she must have known innately, somehow, she feels lightened, relieved. Believed. She sobs uncontrollably and the deep chasm of realisation opens within her. The demons shriek from within, their claws clutching at her heart. Elle snarls at them and says, *No, not now. Not yet.* And the black shadows vanish into the night air.

She and James sit silently in this calm moment of solidarity. There is a stillness between them, a knowing. But this moment is quickly surpassed by a deep rage. The hollow, raw and gaping hole of trauma begins to throb and scream again. The rage, Elle thinks, she only feels when she drinks. With this realisation, suddenly the siblings see each other through different eyes; they see each other's darkness. They endure the fear. They bear the shame.

CHAPTER 25

James—Summer Holidays—2012

Although James does not sleep much that night, the next day swims by with more food, laughter, wine, and beer. James is relieved that everyone is still in party mode; he cannot bear the thought of pretending to be sober. After holding Elle and listening to her cry, James's raw anger at his older brother is seethingly hostile. He pushes aside these dark thoughts and instead downs another cold beer. In the early afternoon, the family clan heads to the beach for a swim and to play frisbee. The water is lukewarm and full of seaweed, but nobody cares. Mick and Stacey stand out with their Melbourne tans, and James teases them with taunts of "moon-bakers", wearing their "togs" instead of "cozzies".

After everyone tires of frisbee, Mick and James break away to wander along the coastline, kicking at lumps of cunje and passing the frisbee lazily between their hands.

"So, how are you doing after last night?" asks Mick quietly.

James inhales swiftly and stoops to pick up a shell. He tosses it into the air and catches it again. Looks out to sea. Sighs again.

"I dunno, man," he concedes. "I think part of me always knew. But last night, you know, seeing her like that. Rips my fucking heart out."

"Yeah, I know." Mick keeps up his pace, hesitant to slow down in case James stops talking. Mick found out about the "situation" just over a year earlier, when James was discharged from the army. Mick was a lieutenant at the time, deployed to Darwin to oversee a Marine Rotational Force and suffer in the humidity, tormented by croc-infested waters he couldn't swim in.

When Lance Corporal Laydon was searching for James after he was reported missing by his roommate, Laydon contacted an old mate from their training days at Kapooka, Mick Whitlock, James's cousin.

After an intensive search, James was found unconscious in a grassy field of the Hampstead barracks, way down south in Adelaide. Mick, positioned way up north in Darwin, was powerless to help, but he was able to talk to James's supervisor and convince him to medically discharge James with a DVA pension as opposed to charging James with possession and use of an illegal substance and kicking him to the curb. Mick wonders now whether James ever knew he influenced that decision.

Back on the beach on the insulated Central Coast of New South Wales, James and Mick walk silently along the turquoise shore. Mick remembers a time when he went to stay at Auntie Pearl's house for the school holidays. He must have been, what, maybe ten? That would have meant Elle was eight and James only four.

Auntie Pearl's home backed onto the national park at Koolewong. The house was on poles, with a steep driveway that curled through swaying gum trees and boisterous bracken fern. The young cousins, Elle and Mick, were close. They shared inside jokes and played board games together. Mostly, though, they were outside in the bush, building cubby houses and navigating their way through wallaby tracks up to the ridge and beyond.

It was Mick's third night at his aunt's house, and they were having dinner around a round, wooden table, the laminate scratched by forks over the years of kid-raising, when Pearl said, "I'll be leaving early tomorrow morning to play tennis. Lance will look after you until I get home after lunch." And then she looked at her daughter and her nephew, and said, "I want you two to be good."

Elle inhaled quickly. Mick felt his shoulders tense.

"Okay," they replied in unison.

Across the table, Lance snarled.

Pearl didn't notice.

That night, Elle, James, and Mick were getting ready for bed downstairs, camped out on mattresses on the floor of the second living space. Lance had moved downstairs into a converted bedroom to claim some independence from sharing bunk beds with his sister upstairs in the main part of the house. Since he had moved downstairs, he often used the garage door to sneak out or he played hired arcade games well into the night while Pearl was sleeping. It seemed Pearl had put her trust in Lance now he was a sullen teenager. Pearl had thought back to when she was a teenager, and how sensible and mature she'd been, looking after her five younger siblings and staying far from trouble. Pearl assumed her eldest son was just as responsible and principled. A mother should know best, but in this case, Pearl was terribly off the mark.

"I'm sleeping on that side!" screeched James. His snow-white hair and pudgy face with dimples scowled at his big sister. Elle threw a pillow at him. He barked at her—yes, like a dog. Mick jumped between them and flopped down onto the mattress, spraying his arms out wide and laughing. James jumped on Mick's stomach, which made Mick cough and splutter.

"I want that side!" James sulked again.

"Okay, okay. Fine," conceded Elle. "I'll sleep in the middle and Mick can have that side." She pointed to the edge closest to the garage door, and Lance's room.

After they had cleaned their teeth and kissed Pearl goodnight, the three cousins were side by side and edging close to sleep. James nodded off first, cuddling his pillow. Elle had closed her eyes against the dull hue of the room. Then she heard the familiar sound. The unclicking of Lance's bedroom lock. Her heart jumped and she squeezed Mick's hand.

Mick sat up first. "What?"

Lance stood in the doorway of his room, backlit by a red-and-green lava lamp silhouette. He seemed so much taller and older than Mick. Lance was a lanky thirteen-year-old with a mullet and wearing a too-big Sydney Kings basketball shirt.

Lance took a few steps towards them. Elle was still lying down, curled into a ball, eyes wide but hoping Lance couldn't see her.

"Tomorrow," he growled at them, "tomorrow, you are both fucking dead." And then he went back into his room and locked the door.

Elle could feel Mick's quickened breath when he lay back down.

"Don't worry, cuz, he was just joking," Mick tried to calm Elle, who was starting to cry.

"But, Mick, Mum won't be here." She sobs quietly now. Next to her, James fidgeted, stretched his neck, but stayed asleep.

"That's okay, Ez, I have a plan." And Mick smiled at her.

But Elle did not feel safe. Her cat, Tabby, all fluff and fur, climbed over her legs and settled on her chest, purring as she rubbed his ears. She whispered softly to him, "Please, Tabby, tell me if you see him coming; tell me." Soon both Tabby and Elle fell asleep, nestled between Mick and James.

* * *

Elle remembers the morning air being humid and sticky. Mick remembers the morning as one of survival, a day that he often thinks about in the future when he is working for the armed forces. Mick, Elle, James, and Pearl eat Weet-Bix and sultanas for breakfast. Then Pearl rushes off to get ready for her tennis tournament. James is dropped off at a friend's place to be babysat while Lance, still sleeping downstairs, is cautioned to *look after the kids!* via a note scrawled on a post-it and stuck to the fridge door.

Mick and Elle watch Pearl's car disappear down the steep and curling driveway, blowing soft clouds of smoke from the exhaust. They wave goodbye sadly, but Pearl is watching the road behind her and does not wave back.

Once out of sight, Mick grabs Elle's wrist and pulls her inside, grabs a backpack, hoists it onto his back, and together they dart out the front door and up the side of the house. The home backs onto the national park. They crawl up the stone steps, past the Hills Hoist clothesline, steering to the right where they climb up Big Rock. The kids in Albany Street have names for everything, customs and codes galore. Together they have forged shanties and built teepees, carved paths through the bracken fern, and navigated their way up escarpments to caves and cliff ledges.

Mick and Elle perch themselves atop Big Rock and gaze down at the house they just fled. The red roof tiles slant upwards and then escape down towards the road. The grapevine is in full bloom over the pergola at the rear of the house. Below the dwelling, Elle can see the wavy blue of the pool water and the tall pine tree stretching up above them all.

"I brought us some bread," smiled Mick. He opens the backpack. Inside there are two pieces of wholemeal bread, a plastic water bottle, some rope, and a bottle of Aeroguard.

"Wow! Where are we going?" asks Elle, equal parts excitement and fear vibrating through her tiny frame.

"Let's go up to the ridge. We can hang out in the Red Cave until your mum comes home."

Elle feels a huge sense of relief that Mick has a plan. "Yes, let's just hide away until Mum comes home. Lance won't know where we are. He can't get to us."

With that, Elle and Mick scramble backwards down the greying rock and begin picking their way through the dense bracken fern and grass trees. The ferns are nearly as tall as Elle, but Mick is at least a foot taller than the scrub. They athletically wriggle through the tangle of vines and up the escarpment until they reach a curve in the scrub. Here they swing to the right and help each other up the ridge face and into a more barren terrain. From here they can see all ten houses of Albany St, see their roofs and chimneys, their clotheslines and a couple of cars parked on the street. Beyond the row of homes, they can see the dark blue lake of Brisbane Water. Boats sit on the shore and rock gently in the wind. The sun has risen above the bay and for a moment, all Elle and Mick can hear is the calling of birds and the panting of their own breath.

Suddenly, from atop the ridge and looking down, they see movement and hear a noise. A loud, persistent, mewing noise.

Tabby. *Meow, meow, meow.* He is treading through the underscrub and making his way towards Elle and Mick.

Right behind the cat is Lance.

"Go home, Tabby, go home!" Elle shouts.

Mick grabs her by the arm, heaves his backpack and lurches further into the scrub, dragging Elle with him.

It is two hours before they come back down the ridge. And when they do, they are eight houses up the street and knocking on a sort-of-stranger's door.

"Please, my brother is chasing us and I think he might hurt us if we go home. Can we come in?" Elle pants.

The neighbour, a recently separated thirty-something lady named Michelle who plays netball with Pearl on a Thursday night, says, "Of course, Elle, come in. Do you want some toast?" The kids nod, as they know how to be polite.

An hour later, Michelle calls Pearl.

She says, "The kids are here. They went for a bushwalk and must have gotten lost. Don't worry, they're safe now."

No-one asks the kids about Lance.

CHAPTER 26

James—Still Recovering—2017

James replaces drinking alcohol, smoking meth, and injecting heroin with swallowing pharmaceutical drugs, hurting his body with CrossFit and surfing. After three short stays in a rehabilitation clinic at Kellyville to help him detox from the drugs and alcohol and find the right medications for his anxiety, the DVA agrees to pay for a long-stay rehabilitation centre, Sea Acres at Byron Bay. On his way to Byron Bay, James stays with Elle at her little home on the mid-North Coast.

"You are living my life now, brother," she jokes with him, donning a purple floral maxi dress and standing in her kitchen lined with pots of growing herbs.

James laughs and makes a joke about his flippant consumerism and the pile of takeaway rubbish in his car. It's easy to laugh here, in this space, with his sister who has been in his corner his whole life. She gets it.

But mostly, James's poisonous anxiety grips his heart and makes breathing too difficult. When he is in public, James clenches his fists and takes note of all the exits. His army training comes back to him: identify risks, approach with caution, always have an escape plan. Today, however, he is at Hallidays Point Bakery, trying to order a flat white, and not in the Uruzgan Province clad in camo.

Just breathe, he tells himself, looking at the young girl smiling at him from behind the counter. It's his turn to order. Suddenly the counter feels so far away, yet in just two strides he could be through the front door and leaning on the glass cabinet, casually asking for a coffee. Instead, he stands there, a foot away from the entrance, awkwardly taking up space with his oversized arms and too-small head. An older man steps closer behind him, trying to push James forwards. To the right, a small child squeals and dashes past his legs, the mother shouting- *Harry!* James starts to sweat.

Large flat white, with honey. Large flat white, with honey. Large flat white, with honey. The words are there in his head, but his lips won't form them. The girl behind the counter isn't smiling anymore and instead, she is clicking the lid of her pen. *Click, click, click.* Behind her, two white-aproned chefs are moving around stainless-steel trays, one holding meat pies and the other poppy-seed buns. The lights above are fluorescent and they burn down; the one to the left is duller than the others. James hears the child squealing, the mother shouting, the pen clicking, the trays clinking, the man shuffling.

Instinctively, James turns and races back to the car park, his long limbs carving through the crowd. He pushes in front of a trolley that has turned the corner and it jolts his shin. Ignoring the frustrated *hmph* of the permed-haired driver, he trots to the bush that lines the shopping centre and suddenly, lacking any control, throws up on the grass. It stings his throat and nostrils. Leaning on his knees, James breathes heavily and waits for the nausea to recede.

Looking down at the mess, he sees yellow bile and two benzodiazepines half-dissolved.

Man, he really wants that coffee.

* * *

When James finally arrives at Byron Bay, the staff at Sea Acres welcome him with warm and non-judgemental smiles. His initial nerves and social anxiety subside as he is whisked through the check-in process and given a tour of the facility. It is surrounded by lush greenery and nestled between the swaying palm fronds and bamboo, the bone-white villas standing stoically, clad with grainy timber and welcoming name frames like *Serenity* and *Bodhi2*. His guide and soon-to-become mentor, case manager, and closest friend, Gabe, leads the way down a cobbled path and points to a villa where James will spend the next three months. The name in the timber frame next to the door reads *Amara*. From the verandah, James can smell the salty air washing over him. Dropping his bags off and having a quick peek around the abode, James allows Gabe to shower him with reassurances that he is in the right place, and the light inside James agrees. There is a solace in this space that he has not felt for a while.

Over the following week, James falls into the flow of the rehabilitation programme. Gabe is quick-witted and shares James's taste in music. They form a bond quickly, sharing yarns over cups of tea and games of chess. James recognises that it is Gabe's job to be his mate, but likes to think that it is a genuine friendship. There is a familiarity about his oval-shaped tanned face and curly ash-blonde hair, slightly crooked teeth, and jutting jawline, with a height that matches James's stature. They talk about CrossFit and surfing. Gabe suggests he show James some great point breaks when he is feeling better. Maybe he reminds James of his childhood mate, Harley.

Among the other residents—*patients*—James quickly establishes himself as the joker, the funny guy with the big muscles. He enjoys the attention of his peers and the support people, and after two months of rehabilitation, meetings, counselling, equine therapy, massage, whole foods, yoga, and meditation, James earns privileges such as days out with longer hours for surfing. He is feeling strong and capable. Others have not been as successful, and James has had to say goodbye to mates he made in the recovery programme. Mates who could not handle the intense and harrowing group therapy. Mates who couldn't hide from their demons. And in here, they all have demons.

The routine at Sea Acres suits James well. The chaperoned dawn patrol to the beach for yoga and a swim, and then back to the hall for a protein-rich breakfast. Circle time where he jots ideas in his gratitude journal. Quiet time patting the horses and cleaning their hooves for equine therapy. Counselling sessions where muscle-shirt Dan looks him in the eye and nods frequently, making James feel heard and validated. In the afternoon James goes surfing—mostly with Gabe or another resident who needs to wet their gills–and returns in time for a shower and dinner. And lastly, the day ends with a group session where the other *guests* share their successes of this day and their goals for the following day.

"We have a family day coming up." Dan, James's counsellor, hands him a flyer and asks who he will invite.

"Um, Mum for sure. She'll come." James nods enthusiastically.

"What about your dad?" prompts Dan, minutely raising his brows.

Pause. A really long pause.

Thinking back to the last conversation with his father, where words once spoken—or yelled—could never be retracted, James leans back in his chair. It was during one of James's benders, and after coming down, he was isolated in Sydney, without a place to stay. He called Simon from a pay phone, even though his speech was slurred and unsteady. Simon answered, trepidation in his tone. In a deep depression and vague of mind after two weeks of using meth and oxy, James begged Simon to come and pick him up—*please*—and let him stay a while so he could gather himself. Simon was unsympathetic and said something about how James should call again sometime "when you are sober". There was more distressed begging from James, more staunch resistance from Simon. Words like "druggo", "poor character", and "dole bludger" were thrown around by Simon, and James countered with phrases like "useless father", "you've never cared", and "you're dead to me". Eventually, Simon hung up—as though that would fix the problem—leaving James swaying in the cold with a tear-streaked face, sunken eyes, and papery skin, slamming the receiver on the phone box in a desperate display of helplessness.

No money. No food for days. James couldn't remember where he'd left his duffel bag. His dad lived only kilometres from where he now slumped, emotionally and physically exhausted.

Shaking his head at the memory and realising Dan is still waiting for a response, James breathes, "Um, I'll ask. Maybe Dad will come."

"Yeah, okay. Definitely reach out and ask him. It's an important step in your rehabilitation and healing journey, James. I think your mum and dad would be so proud of how far you have come and what you are working through." Dan clicks his pen and closes the notebook on his lap.

"Yeah." James smiles, outwardly.

* * *

After three months at Sea Acres, James is discharged into a halfway house with three other people in various stages of recovery. During the two years at iconic Byron Bay, on Bundjalung Country, James is kicking goals and slaying his demons. Finally, he has clarity, purpose, positive intentions, and a healthy body and mind. He attends NA or AA meetings every day, obtaining his badges and being held accountable for his sobriety.

James remembers his first AA meeting with such clarity. He now has the confidence to open the meetings himself, trusted with the keys to open the church. In the early days at Sea Acres, it was Gabe who spoke of the compulsory twice-a-day meetings, and he wasn't lying.

Loaded into an unsigned minibus, twelve residents, Gabe, and another case worker who was driving ventured into the township for a 3 pm meeting. Held at the Uniting Church—James had never been to church—people milled about near the front entrance as though they were at a party. Everyone seemed to know one another, offering high fives, slaps on the back, and warm embraces. They shared smokes and laughed out loud at something James couldn't hear. He stood awkwardly at the back of the pack, fiddling with a cigarette he had yet to light. Cigarettes were contraband at Sea Acres, but they were easy to locate if one knew the right people. And drug addicts always know the right people.

Standing behind the crowd, James must have stood out. A large man who introduced himself as "seven years sober" asked him what his name was and how he was feeling.

"James. Yeah, good thanks, mate." Kicking at the dirt.

"Come in," Seven-Years-Sober said.

The crowd followed and suddenly the church was full, at least sixty people. James found a wooden seat at the back of the room and tried to calm his nerves by scratching at his forearm. Sometimes, digging his fingernails into his skin would make him more present.

The meeting opened with Seven-Years-Sober on stage, microphone in hand. He introduced himself again.

"My name is Stan, and by the grace of God, I have been sober for seven years." His voice was gruff, his greying hair tousled over a broad forehead.

"Hi, Stan," the crowd echoed in unison.

James looked around but no-one was watching him. He listened to Stan tell his story of drug addiction, the car accident that killed his best friend, his time in lock-up, his path to finding God, his road to recovery, and to this moment. This moment here.

Other people volunteered their stories, courageously taking the microphone and speaking for five minutes—Stan had a timer in his hand—about their experiences. With each story, something resonated with James. He felt the heartache. He remembered the insatiable longing for the next hit. How the weed was good, but the alcohol was better, and when the alcohol stopped working, the heroin was the saviour. He teared up when someone spoke of losing his wife and kids. All of these stories, these humans, were interconnected through their grief, loss, shame, and vulnerability.

Suddenly, Stan was calling on James. *No, no, no.* Sinking into the chair, the room started to sway.

"James, we haven't seen you here before. Come on up and tell us a bit about what brings you here today." Smiling, arms wide as though waiting for a hug, Seven-Years-Sober waited.

"Um, no thanks," James whispered, barely audible. People twitched and shuffled in their seats. James waited for Stan to call on someone else, but the next seconds felt like he was back in Afghanistan. The stillness of anticipation. Trying to find his breath in his chest. Assessing the imminent threat.

"*Jaaaaames!*" boomed seven-years-sober-Stan from the front of the room.

Like the soldier that he was, reacting to the directive, James stood up, tunnel-visioned and seeing the room through blurry eyes, catching his breath in his chest, exhaling deeply. *Move, Gunner James Bartelle, move.* He marched to the front of the room, every strange face watching each step.

Stan shouted into the microphone, "Now *that*, everyone, *that* is courage!"

The crowd cheered and someone whistled.

Somewhat encouraged, James climbed the steps onto the stage, took the microphone, and stared out at the sea of eyes.

"Hey, I'm James and I'm an alcoholic." He swayed a little.

"Hi, James." Again, a wave of audio echoed through the hall.

James looked to his left at Stan for some guidance, and the big man smiled kindly, motioning with his hands to keep going, offering a thumbs-up for reassurance.

Gazing back over the mob of strangers, James caught Gabe's face in the front row so he decided to speak to him, trying to forget about the other fifty-eight people in the room.

"Um, yeah. So, I uh, I moved up from Sydney. I was in the army before that. Served in Afghanistan a couple of years back. When I got home, I was struggling a fair bit. Started drinking more and then um, misusing benzos and then um, I started using meth. Um, what brought me here?" Pausing to search Gabe's face for signs he was on the right track. A slight eyebrow raise, and Gabe's lip turned up at one corner. James continued, "I think I realised I had to change something or else the drugs would kill me. So yeah, here I am. Here I am, and I am eight days sober."

The crowd clapped loudly. Relieved he did not pass out on stage, James handed back the microphone, and Stan surprised him with a strong bear hug.

After this first experience, each meeting became a little easier, with James becoming a little more vulnerable, with a little more to divulge. Amid Gabe's encouragement and the familiar faces like Stan's, James began to find his voice, take some responsibility, look his demons in the eye, and started to feel a connection with other people instead of with the bottle.

* * *

Life is good. James has found solace at Byron, surfing, playing mixed netball, chasing waterfalls, and CrossFit training. One day, as had become their ritual, James and Gabe went for an early morning surf. They rose before the sun had cracked the horizon and loaded their longboards into Gabe's wagon. The car chugged down the midnight-blue road that ran parallel to the iconic Byron Bay Main Beach. Gabe checked in on James, asking him how his night was, what he was looking forward to that day, and the usual questions he asked as a case manager and now mate. James was honest and confessed he was feeling really well-charged and strong in himself.

Gabe suggested they check the waves at Wategos, and so the car weaved its way up and over the hill, between the bat's wing ferns and swooping Bangalow palms. The sky was turning inky orange, burnt like the embers of a long-lasting campfire. James wound down his window and breathed in the humid, salty air.

Arriving at Wategos Beach, the pair squeezed into their wetsuits, waxed their boards and ran for the sparkling water, now a teal ocean with the eyes of Mother Sunshine looking at them over the horizon. The break was tidy and clean, the swell not too big. James paddled hard towards the rising sun, past the breakers, and sat on top of his board. A soothing warmth washed over his face as the sun climbed higher. James sat, not surfing, but drifting in the sea. His feet swirled small circles below the board, just enough to keep the buoyancy and rhythm of his meditation, although he did not call it a meditation, then. If someone—Gabe—had said that the morning surf was a mediation, James would have laughed out loud and then grimaced at the word. But in years to come, when James is sober again, he will look back on this moment as significant.

He allowed the board to hold him, allowed Mother Blue to wrap her salty limbs around his body and hold him safe in her embrace. For what could have been half an hour, James watched the sun rise and listened to the sea birds make their pilgrimage from land to ocean. He smelt the salt and seaweed and the summer morning air. James closed his eyes and thought, for the first time since he'd started recovery, that he was doing alright. He told himself he was doing this. He was actually doing this sobriety. And fuck, it felt amazing.

Later that day, Gabe would tell James what he saw: A healed man sitting with his eyes closed and looking completely at peace.

At peace. Those are the words that James will remember about that particular surf. At that particular moment in time, at peace. That precious, drop-in-the-ocean-picturesque-solitude-moment in time. Peace.

* * *

With all of the exercise, sunshine, and whole-food eating, James had never looked so good. When his counsellor asked him why he went to the gym so often, he replied, "So I look good naked." The counsellor laughed at James's candour and congratulated him for finding a healthy outlet for his addiction.

"Because," he adds, "after all, we are all addicts. It's just that some addictions are healthier than others."

Feeling proud and worthy again, James smiled easily and did not feel threatened by compliments anymore.

But he does not exude this confidence around girls. Anxiety still stops him from dating. The thought of sitting down at a restaurant and making small talk and wondering whether she likes him or not sends his head into a spin and his palms begin to sweat. This is, of course, until he meets Lily.

Until that fateful and serendipitous massage from the elegant Lily, James has to keep his body moving in order to stay on the recovery train.

Once he has finished the long-term rehab at Sea Acres, he moves into a halfway house at Byron, where there is support and accountability in the form of fortnightly drug and alcohol testing. Once James reclaims his independence and proves to himself and Gabe that he is capable of functioning as a law-abiding citizen without mind-altering substances, James takes out his own lease on a tidy villa by the seaside—subsidised by the DVA, of course.

Now establishing his own routine, he gives up meditation—*thank God*—as it is no longer part of his mandatory programme. Focusing on his breath actually made him more anxious, as though his heart were a pulsating time bomb, ready to explode like a nail bomb in Kabul. He felt patronised by the social workers who insisted on mediation and mindfulness. There is nothing that could truly transcend the horrors of war. James's nervous energy would ripple through his body.

No longer holding a weapon in the middle of the Afghan desert or snorting a line of meth, he feeds his need for thrills by finding crooked cliffs to climb and unforgiving waves to surf. He thrives on the adrenaline rush. It is the only way he can keep his mind from wandering down the prickly path of his past.

After attending the NA and AA meetings, he would find waterfalls hidden in the hinterland. Climbing steep mountains and jumping from the rock face into the chilling, murky water below. Or, if the swell was favourable and there were waves, he paddled hard and fast straight into the breakers and let the water churn over his body. The rush.

But also, somewhere deep inside, if he really searched, there was a little voice that told him, *Who cares if there is a rock just under the surface of this waterhole? Who cares if a Great White is lurking around the point at dusk?* James takes the risks without thinking the consequences are that big of a deal. Sober or not sober, this is how he lives his life. For the rush.

And James manages to stay sober for nearly two years.

CHAPTER 27

James—Money—2019

James checks his account for the fifteenth time that day and it is only 10:07 am. His breath catches in his throat when he sees the numbers. So many numbers. He reads the digits over and over. *$234,012.78.*

James picks up his phone and texts Lily.

Pack ur bag babe. Tell work you wnt b there all wk.

She texts back with a purple heart emoji and a yellow smiley face with white hands that look to be flapping in excitement. In his apartment, James is also flapping his arms around, gyrating his hips, punching the air. He lights another smoke. Finally, he can breathe. Since successfully finishing his treatment and proving to himself and everyone around him that he can live in sobriety, he has been living on a DVA pension, about sixteen hundred dollars a fortnight. It is just enough to cover his subsidised rent, his CrossFit and gym memberships, the high-protein Muscle Chef meals he has delivered to his home, and his addiction to fast fashion and takeaway coffees. Looking at his bank account, James sighs deeply, knowing he does not have to take on that fencing job for two hundred dollars a day that some surfing mate suggested he have a go at. Now he can buy that vintage longboard he's had his eye on, and the new trainers—fuck, he can buy two pairs: one in black and the other in yellow.

He has never had much money. Reflectively, James ponders the times he played poker with his dad and sister, using twenty-cent pieces as tokens. James was probably seven or eight and just learning the coins and numbers. It was fun, winning and losing the stack of coins. He would build his pile up in a tower, and then watch as it toppled over, laughing. His dad would throw a huge, expensive bet, and put all of his coins in the middle. James would always match the bet, never folding, because he loved the look on his dad's face, mock shock with twinkling mischief in his eyes. These are probably James's first lessons in money management. Poker and Monopoly. Closely followed by the way his mum would never give him money. When Pearl dragged him to go shopping at the supermarket, she would only buy no-brand food and specials. James was never given pocket money like the other kids in the street. And it did not help that Dad pointed out at every opportunity how "poor and tight your mum is". Eight-year-old James nodded in agreement and rolled his eyes the way that always made Dad smile. The juxtaposition between the lavish weekends with his dad and the long penny-pinching school weeks with his mum glaringly cemented who he would rather be like.

Now he is thirty-two and he does not have much to show for himself other than a stack of material possessions and memories of loose nights. His sobriety has meant he doesn't waste his pension on drugs and booze, but he always spends his money, never saving.

But all that doesn't matter now–he has a quarter of a million dollars and he can spend it on whatever the fuck he likes.

James opens his laptop and searches for places to stay at Blue Mountains. He had met Lily a few months earlier and the spark between them was instant. He had felt safe enough to tell her about his time in Afghanistan, and the downward spiral into using alcohol and drugs, his stints in rehab. As he'd spoken courageously about the last eighteen months of his sobriety, he could see how proud she was of him. Lily was cool with it all, not a single bit judgy, and he was smitten.

Recently, Lily opened up to James about her childhood memories of staying with her nan at Katoomba and how devastated she was when her nan sold the house and moved into a nursing home. James watched as Lily's face crumbled while speaking of the huge verandah that wrapped around the timber home, dressed in bougainvillaea and wisteria. While Lily's nan thought the home was run down and "no-one comes to help me anymore", seven-year-old Lily saw the overgrowth as enchanting and magical. She would search for fairies and ladybugs within the thorny brambles, collecting the pink and purple flowers from the vines to create potions for her spells. The emerald moss growing on the north end of the verandah, while a slip hazard for old Nan, created a soft and spongy play space for Lily's figurine horses who danced and twirled in the dappled sunlight. There weren't any young children in the cul-de-sac of the leafy Katoomba home, and her nan seemed too old to play, so Lily spent hours indulging her imagination with tales of heroism and adventure.

James clicks on a link and fishes out his debit card. Smiles again when he remembers all of those numbers in his bank account.

He thinks of all of those digits lined up in his savings account and is reminded of the soldiers in his battalion, lined up diligently in sandy-coloured camo at Tarin Kowt Base Camp. The waiting helicopter buzzing, impatient. The acrid wind echoing under James's helmet as he awaits the call to embark. The call comes and the soldiers lurch forwards, moving as one unit into the belly of the mechanical monster. Good soldiers, always following command. The chopper roars louder and lunges up vertically into the twilight. It is not long before they reach the drop point and the chopper hovers, lowers. The soldiers are signalled to disembark, to land softly on the desert sand, a simple mission. One by one the gunners crouch, jump, heave their packs, and side-trot to the edge of the clearing, out of the whiplashing wind of the helicopter blades. James is third to reach the meeting spot, and he mills with the other soldiers, rifle in hand. They are outside of a patrol base in the Baluchi Valley, north of the main base at Tarin Kowt. The soldiers have been summoned to assist the personnel with the training of the new Afghan recruits. James has been looking forward to this new adventure, as the C-RAM routine was very repetitive.

The valley is misty and James sees shadows moving in the distance. He cups his eyes and glances again, but the shadows evaporate into dust. Three more soldiers have joined him and are fixing their backpacks, adjusting their helmets. No-one was expecting the sound of gunfire. No-one was expecting Private Havvit-Moore to crumble to the ground, inky blood squirting from his chest, eyes wide with surprise. James drops to the ground and rolls away to the edge of the dune, swallowing dust and choking as he hears two, three more blasts.

Shaking away the memory, James remembers the numbers in his bank account. The compensation. A quarter of a million dollars to say *Sorry we dropped you in the wrong place, but please do not tell anyone.* James is angry with Private Havvit-Moore. He is angry that he died right there in front of him on what should have been a conflict-free mission. Late at night when he can't sleep, James imagines all the other outcomes that could have, should have been. He conjures the spirit of Havvit-Moore and speaks to him, telling him that he is sorry.

But the money helps. James isn't going to pretend the money doesn't make him happy.

* * *

Lily and James fly business class from Brisbane to Sydney, where James hails a taxi and pays the driver cash to take them to the sleek

Inyanga Retreat perched on Owen Mountain, a sultry haven of seduction and promising deep, cellular restoration. The lighting is soft and the earthen textures ground Lily, making James smile as Lily pads barefooted along the cobblestoned floor. Their room is the best in the resort. They will spend a week here, connecting with the earth, the mountain, and each other.

Clad in white robes, the lovers enjoy massages in their room, dine on room service, and make love in the sauna. While this style of holiday is not what Lily is used to, nor James, Lily tells James she loves him, and that makes the exorbitant spending worth every cent.

James has been sober for nearly two years. The two years have been filled with clarity and focus. James has been centred on health and wellbeing, reigniting his connection with the sea and his muscled body. But tonight, mesmerised by Lily's angelic beauty, he feels stronger than ever. Tonight, here in the mystical mountains of the Snowy Ranges, he feels worthy of love. Despite not knowing Lily for all that long, he knows that the hard work he has invested over the past two years entitles him to something magical. All of his suffering, all of James's dedication to staying sober, means he should be rewarded. And anyway, he doesn't want to seem boring or immature in the presence of his lover, so James confidently orders the most expensive bottle of red wine and the whole lobster—he doesn't even like lobster—and Lily appears to appreciate the gesture and she daintily picks at the spread of indulgence.

James stares at the opened bottle of wine and considers his commendable strength, his ability to abstain for nearly two whole freaking years. He hesitates while he thinks of his sponsor, Gabe, who would, of course, answer the phone if only James had the momentary insight to stand up from the table, walk away, and make the bloody phone call. Watching the bottle perched in the middle of the white linen-clad table, James's hand is twitching under the table on his bouncing knee. James is alone with his inner torment as Lily smiles awkwardly at him and sips her wine, candlelight flickering in her eyes. James waits for her to say something, but realises she probably has no idea what to say. Twenty-three is synonymous with naivety. Relief floods through James's body.

He swallows his hesitation and reaches for the shiny and smooth wine glass, stroking the cool glass stem. Seizing the bottle with his other hand, he tilts and pours—just a mouthful—into the glass. Yes, he convinces himself, a mouthful will be fine. A mouthful to seem polite. He will only have a mouthful.

The warm peppery flavour fills his mouth, his throat. A burning desire, like the edge of a climax. He swallows the first sip. Closes his eyes and savours the taste. Grins. The first sip is quickly followed by a larger mouthful, and the glass is now empty. A whole-body experience, a surging benevolence undulates down his chest, through his limbs, and suddenly he feels like he is flying. James inhales deeply as the wine reminds him of good times and freedom. Smiling across the table at Lily, James pours another glass, this time much more than a mouthful. They talk and laugh about the day, rubbing their feet together under the table. As the glass empties, James finds himself no longer laughing with Lily, but laughing along with his dear old friend in a bottle he has not seen for two dry and flavourless years.

Ironically, Inyanga is named after a South African term meaning "healer" or "herbalist". In years to come, James will look back at this moment and realise that Inyanga did not heal him; rather, in a moment of excitement—weakness—he dropped his guard and chose to rip the scar tissue open. The lavishness, the opulence, and the seduction all made James susceptible, and he chose to feed his addiction once more, refilling his empty glass.

Until now, James has been grateful for the support of the Department of Veterans Affairs. His case manager and his rehab mentor have been nothing but helpful, responding to his requests for accommodation support, assisted transport to and from appointments, and the fortnightly pension he receives. James cannot imagine working again, between the recurring pain in his shoulder, his crippling social anxiety, and his inability to commit to a full-time job, meaning his only form of financial survival is the handout he receives from the government. James deserves these payouts; he suffered while serving his country. His shoulder joint was severed while hoisting the equipment for the rocket across the desert. The nightmares of his childhood and teenage years returned as he sat hunched in the underground bunker in Afghanistan, staring at a computer screen for hours at a time, night after night of interrupted sleep. Gunner James Bartelle was working—serving his country, goddammit!—when a truck full of dead and dying bodies was dumped at the base camp, and he lugged severed arms and pieces of rib cage from the dust to the first aid tent, unsure if he was screaming or if it was someone else. Gunner James Bartelle was standing in the shadows the night his comrade was shot.

Yes, civilian James deserves the recognition for his trauma. He deserves the lifetime of psychological support, the subsidised medication, the weekly pension.

With a quarter of a million dollars in his bank account, James is elated. He can do whatever he wants. He starts with drinking expensive wine with the love of his life in an exclusive resort. Then, he books two flights to Vietnam, business class.

Within eight months, in the midst of a global pandemic, James will be broke again. He will be cash-broke, love-broke, health-broke. Broken.

CHAPTER 28

Elle—Money—2019

Her quiet life on Biripi Country with Bryce is peaceful. Elle is in a nice flow, moving through her yoga practice each morning, finding a rhythm in her breath. The anxiety of her twenties is a memory of the past and Elle is proud of herself for growing into a calm and balanced adult. She enjoys Bryce's tranquil energy and the way he wanders the garden, tenderly touching leaves and taking photos of intricate flowers that he shows to her over dinner. Elle does not care much for gardening, but she is proud of what Bryce has created in their backyard.

The world is about to change, but Elle and Bryce will remain mostly untouched by the global pandemic. Mostly. Only time will tell just how history will remember the years of 2020 and 2021. But for now, Elle is unperturbed by global affairs.

She is worried about her brother. It has been a few weeks since he answered her calls, and as experience tells her, this means he has slipped off the sober train. She worries about what will become of him, dreading a phone call without a happy ending. Elle's life is settled and simplistic, and she deserves this, after the chaos and drama of the years prior. But with James still struggling with his addiction and the deep resentment he has towards Lance, Elle cannot completely relax until she knows James is safe. She tries to call him again, but it rings out, and she hears his message service asking her to say a few words after the beep.

Bryce and Elle bought their house in the country a few years ago, in a rural community where house prices were manageable. Their comfortable three-bedroom home with a pool perches on a hill, overlooking farming land. With his qualifications in permaculture, Bryce took great pride in designing their yard with principles of working with nature, instead of against it. There is a banana circle in the middle, with the grey water from the shower feeding into it. The happy banana family provides year-round fruit. Further down the sloping block, Bryce used his sweat and manpower to form swales in the land so the water catches in trenches and runs like a muddy water slide along the rows of fruit trees. There are over sixty varieties of trees, from Panama berry and avocado to black sapote. The diversity of plant life attracts a flock of colourful birds who feast on the surplus. The bees and the butterflies swarm the array of rainbow blooms and Elle is forever swatting mosquitoes and spiders who sneak their way from the garden into the home.

It is December 2019, and Elle is watching the morning news while lemon verbena tea brews in the kitchen. There is a report on a virus spreading in China. She watches with feigned interest and turns the television off, already feeling the uncomfortable stickiness of humidity. Back in the kitchen, Elle fills her cup with scalding tea and watches the trees in her backyard sway and dance in the wind, taking a moment to feel deep gratitude for all she has, for the space and the life that grows within. She touches her belly, connects to the swollen hardness of her womb pushing against her stretched skin. The inner world meeting the outer world. She feels the baby roll and, momentarily, Elle ponders what life will be like for this child. Feeling protective, she rubs her belly and whispers, "You are so loved, and so very safe", and wants to believe her own words.

In the distance, out past the orchid and the bushy bamboo lining the back fence, past the roofs of neighbouring homes and up the side of the mountain, she watches it. The wind blows harder, a hot and suffocating heat consuming the countryside. On the mountain, curling up into the sky, thick brown smoke billows. Knowing that, behind her, the parched mountain to the north has also burnt to embers and now the mountain to the east is also on fire, Elle sighs, concerned. This summer has been called Black Summer by the media giants, and it is really all people are talking about. Homes across the state have been lost, and the fires have been savage walls of unrelenting fury. Elle and Bryce have spoken at length about the drought over the past two years, and how the land has been ripped and cleared of the trees needed to hold the topsoil. Without the topsoil, the grasses and saplings cannot grow as they are whisked away with each breath of wind. The farmers have been allowed to clear thousands of hectares for their grazing cattle, raping the land of nutrients and soil needed for a healthy ecosystem. After two years of drought, the land is exceptionally dry. Now, with unprecedented weather patterns, thousands of hectares are burning, animals dying and homes destroyed.

She rubs her belly and whispers to her baby again, who is now a week overdue. "It is safe for you to arrive." Yet Elle knows that the words she whispers are not the truth the baby hears.

Later that day, lounging under the fan in the overwhelming heat of the summer, watching a trashy reality television show, Elle is surprised when her phone rings and even more surprised that it is James. As she answers, it is with trepidation.

"Hey, Ez." He sounds elated and upbeat.

Elle sighs with relief.

"Where are you, Jay?"

"Aw, Lily and I are in the Blue Mountains. We just had an epic massage with hot rocks. And now we're waiting for some new pillows, as the other ones were too hard." James speaks quickly.

Elle's relief at hearing his voice dissipates and the pit of worry and concern returns. She asks her brother a few questions and discerns that the lovers are on a romantic getaway and James is lavishly spending, and quite possibly high.

"Ez, I have to tell you something," James confides. "It's the DVA—they've paid out that compo claim I was telling you about."

Elle recalls a few months ago when James revealed a terrifying account of a disaster while he served in Afghanistan. It was rare for her brother to talk about his time in service, but he spoke with clarity and confidence, and Elle deduced that James's sobriety was allowing him to open up about the issues sleeping underneath his addiction. While she was grateful he was finally confiding in her, she was perturbed by the horrors he'd witnessed.

"Yeah, I remember," Elle assures him.

"Well, the money came through and it was more than what I thought it would be."

"How much?"

The phone is muffled as James speaks inaudibly to someone in the background. She hears him laugh before he returns to their conversation, apologises quickly, and continues.

"Tell me, Ez, how much would you need to make your life more comfortable? Like, give me a figure." James is smiling—Elle can hear it in his voice. She is acutely reminded of the time he handed her two chocolate bars and then offhandedly said sorry for crashing her car. It was a few years ago, after he had been discharged from the military and he didn't have his own set of wheels. She had allowed him to borrow hers while they holidayed at Pearl's place. James was often sneaking out, saying he was checking the surf. The flippancy of his confession is reminiscent of this moment now. Elle is unsure what to say but gives him a modest figure.

"I don't know; probably ten K would pay our bills and we could finish the deck out the front and put in a new air conditioner.

It's really bloody hot here." She twists a strand of hair around her index finger and watches it curl and unfurl.

"Mmm, yeah, I bet it is," James says, and the conversation moves away from money and onto the weather, the brutality of the bushfires, James's and Lily's upcoming holiday to Vietnam. He is excited and bubbly and Elle wants to be happy for him. But she can't ignore the imprinted feeling of being wary. While James sounds coherent over the hundreds of kilometres of cellular waves, he also sounds borderline manic. Elle can hear how the inflection at the end of each sentence is speeding up and quickening with excitement. His words mash together into a feeding frenzy of sentences. Eventually ending the call with "I love you" and "Let's speak before I fly overseas", Elle lolls backwards onto the lounge, arm resting on her balloon belly with sweat beading on her forehead. Exhausted.

What a summer, she thinks. Any moment now, her and Bryce's lives will change with the addition of an innocent and wholly dependent baby, in the midst of the worst bushfire season in New South Wales on record, and the world being on the cusp of a global pandemic, all of which will alter the course of their future. For now, naively and serenely ignorant, Elle closes her eyes and rests.

The next day Elle is shocked when she notices fourteen thousand dollars in her bank account. Trembling with jubilation, Elle calls James to say thank you. She calls him three times, but he does not answer.

CHAPTER 29

James—Vietnam—2020

Lily is not sure what to do this time. James has been gone for nearly two hours. She sits in the bungalow, watching the horizon and the waves lapping against the grey sand. Lily thought this time in Vietnam would be magical, like the first six months of their relationship. Somehow, she thought James would be kinder, softer, gentler, more sober. The medication he is on seems to plateau his moods, but he is drinking more, so much so that he had emptied the mini bar and left the resort in search of replenishing the stock—now two hours ago.

At twenty-three years old, Lily had never met someone quite like James. The first time they met, she arrived at his townhouse in Byron Bay to give a remedial massage, as per her employment criteria. It was a Thursday afternoon and the Lawson Street unit was dimly lit, a silver Commodore with a blanketed longboard strapped to the roof sitting idle in the driveway. She squeezed past the car and knocked confidently on the screen door, the sounds of easy-listening music echoing from inside.

Lily was a professional, as she had successfully achieved her Certificate IV in Massage Therapy through Evolve College the year before. She told her friend Maddy how "the course was intense and soooo rewarding". Lily loved how strong her hands became, how small her frame was, how she could create such "intense energy" in a room. Her mum, Daphne, was also a healer—a nurse. A mental health nurse, to be exact. Lily had grown up hearing stories of how and why her mum helped people, how the patients reacted to her gentleness and kindness. Lily pondered how sad it was that her mum drank so much and had divorced her dad and never fallen in love again. Her downhill spiral must have been because all the energy Daphne had given to others meant she had little for herself.

Lily had fallen for James's quick wit and long stories. He was funny and charming. James invited her surfing and they met at dawn, coffees in hand, and fell in love under the close eye of the rising sun. From that day, they were inseparable. James was adventurous and spontaneous. He whisked her away to chase waterfalls, jump off cliffs into the ocean, take road trips to Sydney, and attend parties at Surfers Paradise. James and Lily were electric together. Lily heard all about James's travels abroad and the troubles he found himself in. He told her about rehab and the army. He told her about his family, the love and the pain. Lily shared her story as well, but at twenty-three, her life had consisted of growing up outside of Byron in a small community, finishing school in Year 10, working at a flower farm, and living in a bright orange caravan on the edge of a commune. Lily loved the outdoors and she floated her way through life, like a leaf in the wind. She was graceful, softly spoken, and so damn beautiful.

A year after they met, James received a second large payout from a DVA claim for the shoulder injury he'd sustained while working, and later, serving his country. The recurring pain and trouble he had with the shoulder that was dislocated during training hindered James's ability to work with his hands in any sort of labouring job. He applied for a compensation claim after the near-drowning experience at Lennox Head. It was late afternoon and James had checked all of his local surfing haunts. The swell was messy and closing out in most of the breaks. The clouds were darkening when he decided to paddle out from Boulder Beach, known to the locals as the backside of Lennox Point. James knew that Boulder could hold reasonably big swell and, with its rocky shore and tricky entry points, was not a place for the novice surfer—and James was far from a novice. Filled with adrenaline, he launched himself off the rocks and pushed past the white wash, yearning for a six-foot set to roll in as he reached the far end of the point. Usually, he would have company, but on this particular gloomy afternoon, James had been alone. There were no other surfers braving the wild waves. This beach was usually secluded, anyway.

The first, second, and third waves allowed James to hold himself high on his board, carving sideways along the face before pummelling underneath the unrelenting whitewash, forcing him deep under the surface. It was on the fourth wave—paddling hard to catch the flow—that James felt the familiar pop and sting of his shoulder dislocating itself from the weakened socket. The pain surged through his arm just as the thunderous water hurled his body off the board, wrestling him under and holding him there. Bubbles escaping in a silent scream underwater, James clutched at the leg rope and yanked himself to the surface. In agony, with one working arm, he scrambled onto the surfboard right as another motherfucking wave broke on his head, spinning him around like a piece of seaweed in the wind. Emerging through the water, gasping for breath, tears of pain cascading down his face, James—for once—felt truly terrified. He realised he was powerless against the treacherous and ferocious Mother Blue. Plus the pain in his arm was making it difficult to concentrate, and he was swallowing water, trying to cling to his surfboard, which bobbed like a cork. Towering walls of water crashed around him, their force threatening to engulf him again and again. With each heart-pounding minute, James fought to maintain a hold on the board, attempting to cradle his limp arm, all while keeping his head above water. Struggling for air, James battled against the relentless current, his strength waning.

James does not know how long he was swamped and pummelled in the ocean, but it was long enough for the sky to darken and the wind to howl. It could have been an hour, maybe two. His body had gone into shock from the cold, the pain, and the fear. James's thoughts turned to how, once upon a time, he would have welcomed this moment with gratitude. Once upon a time, he would have surrendered to the waves and allowed himself to be held under, swallowed. That day, however, as James wrestled against Mother Nature, he desperately wanted to survive. All of the hard work of the past eighteen months of recovery, the therapy, the growing acceptance of the demons from his past, and the forward momentum through life, made James cling to his surfboard. Groggily, he remembered how much he wanted to survive, how much he loved nature and travelling—his life would not end now. Not after all he had endured.

Weakly, James apologised to the ocean. His head against the surfboard, body limp in the water, one arm useless and the other wrapped around the fibreglass. He whispered, "I'm sorry I doubted you."

Suddenly, he felt a release, as though the tight fingertips of surging swell had loosened around his waist. There was a lull between the larger waves of the sets—the smaller waves still gliding across the reef. Finding some courage and strength, James kicked his tired feet, kicked his way to the face of the white wash and let himself be shoved to the rocky shore. The sound of a breaker plunging behind him crashed like an avalanche. And still he kicked, the reef slicing and cutting his legs. James thought he heard the ocean crash with a sullen reply, *I'm sorry I doubted you, too.*

When his surfboard crashed onto the shore, James rolled off, face first into the sand. He was coughing weakly, his arm now numb and being held together merely by skin and the material of the wetsuit, every ligament stretched out of place. A lone fisherman, wandering down the beach, saw the dark figure lying there; the water was still licking around James's exhausted body.

* * *

With the thousands of dollars now in his bank account—like playing a board game with free money—he bought a new car, a motorbike, clothes, shoes, a new phone, the best headphones, and of course, showered Lily with gifts. He convinced her to quit her masseuse job and to travel the world with him. Lily could not resist. She sold her caravan, quit her job, said goodbye to her quiet life in Byron Bay, and left with James, but not before saying farewell to her mum. Daphne had squeezed Lily so tightly and whispered in her ear, "Please don't go. Don't give it all up for him." But Lily had shushed her, pecked her on the cheek and said, "Bye, Mumma. And please stop worrying."

Afterwards, Lily told James what had happened and James laughed.

"She is so jealous of you! I bet she is worried you will actually live your life, not like her, stuck at fucking Myocum."

Lily smiled with her mouth, not with eyes, but James did not notice.

Sitting alone in the resort room in Nha Trang, Vietnam, she picks up her phone, switches on the global roaming and starts typing.

20 MAR 2020 9:56PM Lily
Hey Elle. I need your advice … when you have time could you call me?

20 MAR 2020 10:29PM Elle
Hey honey. How are you? Can't call cos Asher sleeping. What's up?

20 MAR 2020 10:41PM Lily

I'm OK. I'm not really sure how you can help, but I think you know James best, and I know he will be cross about me messaging you, behind his back, is how he will see it … but anyway, he's not been feeling good at all and talking about wanting to not exist a lot, getting VERY drunk every day for a while now (which at first didn't faze me because it seemed a better alternative to bashing ice which had been happening for a few days). He's stopped taking his meds but has a lot of valium here … he gets pretty drunk and becomes unreasonably angry and has told me to fuck off back to Australia a few times and I'm struggling to see the light at the end of the tunnel now … sorry to put this on you but I need to share with someone. I don't want to leave him here and I don't think he wants me to leave him at all, but this cycle is continuing … I'm getting worried and I'm not sure how to help.

20 MAR 2020 10:54PM Elle

Thank you for reaching out. It is such a hard situation. I do know James well and I have felt his downhill spiral for some time now. I feel for you. It is not nice to be on the receiving end of his depression and drug abuse. You are right, he probably will get cross that we are chatting but I am very thankful you have contacted me. I'm not sure what I can do, either, other than offer some advice. Please know I love James deeply and only wish him to be happy. I know he needs help. I know he needs to stop drinking for one. Alcohol is his 'trigger' drug. It leads to other, more risky behaviours (as I'm sure you have seen). That being said, we can't click our fingers and he magically stops. Secondly, you really do not deserve to be sworn at or feel put down, and there is NO EXCUSE for his shitty behaviour.

James has had people helping him–family, friends, mentors, psychiatrists–I don't know what the answer is but I wish I did.

Do you want to come home? I'm sure he doesn't want you to leave, but that is absolutely no reason to stay if you don't want to. James needs to be held accountable for his actions, something I don't think has happened enough.

21 MAR 2020 1:08AM Lily
We are still in Vietnam, have found a quiet beach town to chill but he still wakes up feeling shit and feels the only cure is alcohol and what not.

I love him like crazy.

But he's so hard to be around at the moment.

He isn't being himself.

I don't want to leave him. I'm afraid he will do something even more crazy if I go but I don't know if I can handle it anymore.

Lily puts her phone down as she hears James swiping his card at the entryway to the beachside resort. He fumbles and must be holding plastic bags as they crinkle and complain. Bottles clink together. He swears loudly.

Lily jumps up and opens the door for him. Her face is full of concern and she allows a sigh of relief to escape her mouth before she wraps her arms around his sweaty neck. James stands still for a few heartbeats, a gentle sway breaking away from their one-sided embrace. James's hands are full; he can't just drop the bags.

"Hey, Lil," he whimpers. "I'm good, babe. I'm good."

"Yeah, I know," she says and smiles at him.

"I don't want to go home, Lil. Let's stay here forever. You and me. This fucking beach. These cheap-arse drinks!" He raises his voice and lets out a whoop of drunken joy.

Lily runs her fingers through her hair and smiles gently before speaking. "Babe, I want to stay with you, I do. But, you know, the borders are closing. COVID is here. You know the messages we've had from the consulate? They want us to come home. I just don't want to get stuck here, you know?" She takes his bags, and they make their way to the pinstriped daybed that looks across the deserted ocean.

"The army will fly us home if we get stuck. Don't worry, babe, it'll be fine, they can't leave us here."

Lily snuggles into his armpit and crosses her long legs over his. James strokes her hair and they sit like this for a few moments, each staring out into the endless ocean of emptiness, alone in their thoughts but wrapped together with their demons.

CHAPTER 30

Elle—Her Parents Love—2020

A month later, Elle, her newly arrived squishy baby, Asher, and Pearl all have lunch together at a cafe. They speak of the big things and the little things. They both share their concern about James and how he has not been in contact with them as regularly as he used to—before Lily. Elle knows that Pearl desperately wants to protect all of her children and that she can not chase away the feelings of regret and shame that haunt her wherever she goes. Pearl keeps asking, *Where was I? Why didn't I know?* But the answers never come.

After Elle told her mum about Lance's behaviour and the after-effects it was having on her adult life, James quickly followed with his heart-wrenching disclosure. Pearl was dumbfounded and shocked. Disturbed and distressed. As the single parent, primary caregiver, and protector, with her fierce and unconditional love, she carried the burden of responsibility all those years. Unable to shake these feelings of failure and deep contempt for the accusation, Pearl was hurled into a deep pit of clamorous self-doubt and hatred. Following these feelings, Pearl uncovered an unrelenting surge of anger towards her ex-husband, Simon, suppressed for many years as she placated his whims and encouraged her children to have a meaningful relationship with him, despite his faults. Pearl had spent years vanquishing negative thoughts about Simon and conjured positive memories to tell her children, in a selfless attempt to ensure the children loved their father despite the distance and his innate flaws. She could not avoid the feelings of guilt when Ellie or James would cry at night because they missed Simon. Telling stories about holidays spent together in better times and showing photos of them together with their dad, Pearl reinforced the love Simon had for his children and never, not once, planted a seed of negativity. Always defending him, despite her own feelings.

Now—now there is the rage of a scorned woman heaving and hollering.

At the time of the divorce, many, many years ago, Simon walked away so easily, and with such force. Like a shadow in the home, his late-night presence was there one night and had disappeared the next. Pearl had told him that she was unhappy. She asked him to sit and have a conversation about how they could reconnect after years of frayed attachment and finally, the severed connection. But he refused to listen to her. He was angry and heartbroken. All he could see was the red tone of adultery and anything else that slipped from Pearl's mouth was an oily lie. Yet what she had to say was important. There were years of silence and shortcomings between the couple, and Pearl had feelings and insights she wanted to share with her husband. He looked at her with such contempt, lit a cigarette, gulped a shot of whiskey, filled his suitcase with clothes and CDs and shoved his leather work shoes on top of it all. Zipped up the sides and grunted. Stomping down the stairs, Pearl thought Simon might remember the children and stop, returning to kiss their sleeping heads. But he did not stop. He opened the front door, allowing the night air to engulf him and slamming the door in his wake. Pearl remembers how the sound reverberated up the stairwell and punched her in the chest.

The following weeks rushed by in a haze of unanswered questions and confusion. Pearl did her best to maintain a routine and balance in the house and showered the children with cuddles and homemade baked goodies. She noticed Lance was absent most of the time, staying at a friend's place or working. Elle spent less time in her bedroom and instead followed Pearl around offering to help with all of the house duties. While it was endearing, everything took a little bit longer.

After Simon set up his bachelor life in a harbourside unit, he rarely called his family and he never visited the house again. Sure, he agreed to give Pearl the house and he paid child support—for that Pearl was thankful. Other vilified husbands of the nineties refused to pay a cent to their struggling families; Simon was generous with cash and paid Pearl regularly. Yet, more than school shoes and music lessons, the children needed their father's emotional backing. He hardly supported their children, other than with monetary gain and material possessions. Pearl remembers bitterly how Simon did not attend Elle's eighteenth birthday party, and instead sent her a cheque for two thousand dollars. Simon was not present in the audience at James's first musical. Twelve-year-old James had been overwhelmed with excitement, longing to impress his dad. Weeks of rehearsals, singing into the mirror, dressing up, rehearsing his lines with Ellie after dinner. As the matinee drew closer and James had booked second-row tickets for his family, Simon had still not given James a definitive answer as to whether he could make the three-hour journey to visit and watch the show. James held hope, believing his dad would surprise him at the show. But James's anticipation quickly disintegrated into disappointment when the seat he had reserved for his dad remained empty. Afterwards, on the drive home, James cried silently. Pearl could see the glimmery streak down his cheeks as she watched him through the rear-vision mirror. Sadness encased her soul, longing to absorb her son's heartache.

Pearl remembers this moment, and all the other moments, cascading over the years into now, one huge volcano of disappointments, regrets and indignation.

Over ten years of marriage and the addition of three children, Pearl and Simon's relationship had significantly altered. Pearl raised these children on her own. Even in the years that Simon was still living in the same house, he was not present. He was working, reading, or sleeping. And after he moved out in a fury of vindictive accusation, Simon was even less present.

Pearl's ex-husband was not there when Elle was a sulky teenager and she dyed her hair purple, pierced her lip, and chose to wear black spiked belts and blast grunge music from her poster-clad room. He was not there when James was failing his exams and was at risk of being suspended because his apathy towards school work was overshadowed by his desire to have fun in the classroom. Simon was not there when Elle started driving. It was Pearl whose hair grew grey as she explained which pedal was the brake and which was the clutch. He was not there when James had recurring nightmares and wet his bed. It was Pearl who stripped the bed and changed the sheets and tried not to shame her nearly teenage son. Simon was not there when Elle first got her period or when she broke up with her first love and cried red-hot tears for three hours. He did not attend Elle's Year 12 school graduation where she made a moving speech to her peers, nor James's second or third stage performances where he played the leads as Romeo and then Rocky. Simon was not there for the school canteen lunch orders, the fevers in the middle of the night, the tantrums over food they did not like. He was not there for the chaotic rush each morning trying to bundle kids out the door on time *and* with brushed hair, cleaned teeth, and matching socks. He was not there when the children cried because they missed their dad. Pearl spent many hours rubbing their backs, soothing their sobbing, kissing their foreheads, whispering words of love and support. Simon, on the other hand, simply was not there.

And now, after twenty years of single parenting, Pearl is furious.

She calls Simon and declares, through heaving sobs, what Eleanor and James have heartbreakingly disclosed about the truth of Lance as nothing but a fucking animal.

"Where were you?" she hisses. "Where were you when your *favourite* son locked Elle in the fucking cupboard?" Trying desperately to share the overbearing weight of guilt, Pearl's voice shakes.

Annoyingly, Simon silently listens to his emotional ex-wife as she cries and cusses.

* * *

On the other end of the line, Simon sits stoically, stunned and a little stoned. He hopelessly tries to understand the severity of these accusations, but his mind is somewhat foggy and anyway, Pearl can be dramatic. Despite his personal feelings towards his former lover, and of each of his three children, Simon has always felt closest with Lance.

Many years ago, when Pearl cheated with another man, it was Lance who told Simon what he saw one night in his parents' bedroom. Lance saw the silhouette of his naked mother, but the man in the bed was not his father. Angrily, the next day Lance caught the train to Sydney, bursting through the door at Simon's workplace, and started screaming at Simon how much he *hated* his mother. Shocked, Simon listened, and then held his son close, smothering the cries with his expensive woollen jumper.

After the divorce, it was Lance who spent the most time with his father. Simon liked Lance's company—the broody teenage boy with alternative, grungy taste in music. They went to live gigs together and would smoke cigarettes in the corners of the bar. Simon liked Lance's savvy computer skills and together they talked about the rapid changes in technology and culture, as it was the nineties and the internet had just infiltrated society. It wasn't that Simon loved Lance more than his other children, but rather, he simply enjoyed his company more. The adult conversations were easier with Lance–even though he was a young adult–than the childish banter of the younger ones. Lance had a wit that was quick and snippy. Simon felt like Lance was on his side, whereas Ellie and James idolised their mother. As the years went on, Eleanor reminded Simon more and more of Pearl, and he could not help but become short-tempered and judgemental of her actions. But now was not the time to consider the future. Now he was grappling with the fact that two of his children had been sexually assaulted by his eldest son. What to do. Oh, what to do?

Hearing Pearl bombard him with scathing details of Lance's misconduct and her resentment at him for not being around—*How dare she!*—Simon now wonders how much of his children's lives he has really missed. Sadness—no, regret. No, longing—yes—longing for his children's small bodies curled up in his lap, for laughter and games and jokes. For shared Christmases and birthdays and holidays with photos and memories. For school assemblies and late-night popcorn and movies. For not recognising his children's growth spurts until he looked at photos. For all the precious moments he had missed before the world turned sour. Simon longs deeply for the past he was not offered. For the fatherhood of children taken from him, he grieves. What will he do?

First, he calls Lance. Reactive and unprepared, Simon switches into management mode and asks his son, now thirty-four years old, outright.

"What did you do to your brother and sister?"

Lance hesitates before replying. He has a lot to lose.

"You know, Dad, James has a problem with drugs. He doesn't know what he is saying. And Ellie, well, you know she has had that really awful breakup with that dickhead. Maybe she is angry at men and taking it out on me?" Lance sniffs.

Simon takes a sip of his whiskey and lets the information settle in the silence.

Lance murmurs into the phone. "Dad?" he pleads, voice shaking.

Simon exhales a plume of smoke from his cigarette. Watching the lights of the *warang*—harbour—glint in the dim light, remembering Pearl's haunting dramatisation of Lance's predatory behaviour.

"Dad?" Lance's tone is weak and pleading. Childlike.

And then Simon says the same words to Lance that he will to James, many years later.

"Listen, *son*. That is the last time I will call you that. Lance, you are dead to me." And Simon hangs up the phone.

* * *

Mere days later, Simon decides to visit Eleanor. He arrives at her treetop forest house on Worimi Country and she cordially embraces him. The years have softened Simon's business-like authority and he is also softer around the middle, his face shadowed with a greying beard and round-rimmed glasses perched high on his nose. Father and daughter make small talk about the weather and enjoy an afternoon walk around the edge of the lake, which looks murky and grimy. Raff leaps though the shallows, leaving muddy puddles and smiles of joy in his wake.

Over the next twenty-four hours, Simon and Elle will discuss the biggest revelations and speak as honestly as ever before. Between cigarettes on the verandah and refills of red wine, they discuss the intricacies of memories, behaviours, and emotions. Two analytical humans of the same DNA, they decide to compose a spreadsheet of dates, times, places and events–which James will later add to. The spreadsheet will have details of Lance's horrendous actions, the heartbreaking, callous, and calculated deeds that he will no doubt deny. Yet for Elle and James, typing their clear memories into a spreadsheet where it names the place, year, and criminal act, is a timeline like a fault line in the earth. It will be there forever, etched into their minds and under each cell of their body. The data—that's what Simon calls it—will be emailed to Pearl and she will add her timeline in a tidy column that runs down the left of the page.

This considered building of evidence is what Simon needs the most. He has always liked facts and figures and proof. He tells Eleanor to delete the moments when Lance was under eighteen, as "the court will not deem this to be assault", but for her to focus on the significant places and times when Lance was a "knowing, conscious adult". It is hard for Elle to conjure all of the memories and harder still to speak candidly with her father. Yet Simon insists and continues to ask questions and types away into the document, eyebrows furrowed, regularly clearing his throat. Simon needs the truth. He tells his daughter that he wants and longs for justice. For this, Elle is grateful. She did not realise her dad would be quite so supportive. She also did not realise she had been holding in quite so many dark secrets. Her tears fall gently, and internally Elle is apologising to her teenage self. Saying sorry to the little girl who did not scream out for help when she was locked in the cupboard. She forgives silent child Elle, the one who wanted to tell her parents—"Make it stop!"—but was controlled by shame, fear and embarrassment. Now, as she sits with her father as an adult, opening the years of memories and recording them neatly into a document, her inner child wraps her fragile arms around her daddy's neck and feels heard. She feels seen. She feels understood.

Elle knows that over the years of James's addiction, their doting and compassionate mother continues bailing James out of trouble. Elle also knows that her annoyingly forgiving and unpretentious mother continues to send birthday cards to Lance. Pearl hangs his children's artworks in her house. Elle sees the new frames after each milestone and watches her stranger nieces grow by looking at the developing intricacy of their artworks. Like knitting, Elle thinks, Pearl is desperate to keep the threads of the family together, fearing everything will unravel, fall apart and blow away in the wind.

For Pearl's seventieth birthday celebration in 2019, her one wish is to have her whole family together again. After a long conversation and a few post-pregnancy hormonal tears, Elle says she will organise a picnic lunch to mark the turn of another decade in Pearl's life.

"Remember when we used to go to that reserve at Hawkesbury above the marina and have a barbeque with the crew?"

Yes, of course Pearl remembers. She also remembers a frigid night back in 1976, driving at 2 am after she received a phone call to say her dad had died of a suspected heart attack in Brooklyn. He was found in a house by the river, dusty and alone—she doesn't tell Elle these thoughts.

"Yes, Elle, I remember. That sounds like a great place to have lunch."

"Great. Send me a list of who you want to invite and I'll do the rest." Elle is clicking her tongue, already imagining the food menu.

"Elle, I want all of my family there," Pearl says.

Nonchalantly, Elle murmurs, "Of course, Ma, they will all be there." And after they have paid the bill and said farewell, Elle begins to mentally sketch a list of people she thinks should be there to celebrate her wonderful mum.

The celebratory weekend is now only two weeks away. Pearl calls Elle to ask who is coming and mentions–quietly, offhandedly–that she has invited Lance, his wife, Angela, and their two daughters. Elle's blood runs cold and the hairs on her arms bristle. Her breath catches in her chest, threatening to suffocate her while a mending heart thumps loudly underneath her ribs. Elle reaches for the doorframe under where she stands and catches herself mid-sway, world tumbling.

"Mum!" she starts. Where are her words? *Speak, Elle, speak!*

Deep inhale, count to four, hold the breath, exhale for four. Box breathing. In, hold, out, hold. The world around her settles again and Elle can no longer hear her pounding heart echoing in her head.

"I'm sorry, Mum, but if he goes, you know I can't be there." There, the words are there and they linger in the universe.

There is a pause and Elle waits to hear her mum's response. Eventually, Pearl sobs down the line. All Elle feels is deep, entrenched guilt surging through her body; an exhaustion spanning decades.

* * *

Pearl hangs up the phone and lays down on her bed, bringing her knees up to her chest and her cold hands clutch at her mouth. She sobs as she thinks of all the times she has supported her family, her kids, the sacrifices she has made, and now they won't even put their grievances aside for her one wish, for just one day.

A few years ago, in between rehab stints, when James was in a deep depression and self-destructive, Pearl had a phone call from the real estate agent who was seeking permission to conduct a routine inspection. James had sweet-talked the agency into leasing him a brand-new two-bedroom unit, on the banks of Cronulla Beach, with guaranteed rental payment from the generous DVA.

Pearl helped James move. The unit was on the third floor, and the crisp whiteness of the walls and carpet made the blue of the ocean out the front windows dance and hum with undeniable beauty. The ocean commanded their attention, glistening and waving at its new neighbours. James was happy that day, buoyed by the next opportunity to start fresh. He had few possessions, so the move did not take very long. Pearl took James to the supermarket and bought him a hundred and seventy-six dollars worth of groceries.

Weeks later, when the real estate agent called her, Pearl was playing lawn bowls with her girlfriends. She loved playing and was good at it. Lately, though, her attention was split between the bowls, the green, and the worried thoughts in her mind. James was troubled. He had relapsed after seemingly doing so well at the last rehab centre. Pearl knew her son was on a bender because James had not called her for over a week. When he was well, he called her every morning just to chat.

Pearl agreed—on James's behalf—to a routine inspection the following week. The agent sounded grateful and relieved as she had such difficulty getting in contact with "the tenant". Concerned, Pearl tried to track down her son by messaging his friends via Facebook. Hours passed without any luck; she decided to try Instagram and then Snapchat.

Eventually, a woman with an English accent called her, explaining she was a doctor at Sutherland Hospital.

"The police found James Bartelle walking naked through a car park, seemingly intoxicated and delusional. The police brought him to Sutherland Hospital a few hours ago. We have given him a sedative and he is sleeping. He was able to provide his name, and your contact number, but James does not have any other possessions. We are hoping you could come and pick him up as he is nearly ready to leave, please."

Pearl agreed to drive the two hours to Sutherland Shire. Of course she would—she is his mother.

At the hospital, James was thankful to see her. He was wearing a hospital gown and some underwear supplied by the nurses.

Pearl saw her grown son, his eyes gloomy and his skin pale, papery. His hair was greasy and unkempt, a wiry ginger beard covering his chin. She noticed how slim he had become, long gangly arms and pointy knees jolting through the sheets.

After an elongated hug and a few tears, Pearl agreed to buy him some clothes and come back for him to be discharged. James was specific about what he wanted, but Pearl was tired and she did not know if she could find the store Shred Gang. She hoped there was a Lowes or Kmart close by.

After James was dressed and discharged from the hospital, the pair visited the police station to enquire whether his bag had been found. James told Pearl that the last thing he remembered was heaving his army-issued duffle bag through the park, but he felt tired so he lay down to rest. The next thing he remembered was being in an ambulance and going to the hospital. James was confused and irate that someone had stolen his "shit".

At the police station, the Constable shook her head. "Sorry, mate, we haven't had anything turned in with that description."

The next stop was the real estate agent to borrow the spare set of keys. James waited in the car while Pearl tried to fix his life.

The unit was unrecognisable. Clutching at her nose, she asked James, "What is that smell?" He ignored her, pushing past and into the unit, over the clothes, the empty bottles, the cigarette butts, the chicken carcass, the shoes, the DVDs, searching, searching for his bag. James was ranting about someone—"That dickhead with one eye; he stole my shit."

The sudden change in James's demeanour worried Pearl, but not as much as the state of the unit. The once-white carpet was stained with what could be vomit or spilt wine. There were mouldy clothes in the laundry and dirty, filthy dishes stacked on every surface of the kitchen. A hole in the wall between the two bedrooms, about the size of a football, with a broken TV dismembered on the floor below, its cord lolling like the tongue of an exhausted dog.

Eventually, James fell asleep in the lounge and Pearl went about the unit, tidying, scrubbing, washing, and crying.

Back in her room, curled up on her bed, Pearl hears her phone ringing. Composing herself, she dabs at her eyes, straightens her clothes, and answers the call. It is Lance. He is asking her when the party will be, as he needs to make sure he has the time off work.

Pearl swallows, and then she speaks.

"Lance, I'm so sorry, but Elle says you can't come." Pearl cries again. Her heart breaks with every word. Lance begins to swear, calling Elle "crazy" and "selfish".

After he hangs up, Pearl goes back to bed and falls asleep in emotional exhaustion.

* * *

While Pearl is sleeping in her home on the Central Coast, Elle is tending to the needs of her new baby, Asher. He coos and dribbles, like a wrinkled old man, suckling at her nipple. Her partner and lover, Bryce, is outside, chopping firewood. The sudden noise of the axe against timber makes Asher's eyes widen. Elle is peaceful, rocking in an armchair, snuggled in slippers and sweatpants. Things between her and Bryce are settled and calm. Looking around her room, she smiles at the baby equipment and the photos thumbtacked to the dresser. Asher is a happy and untroubled baby, pudgy and bald.

Elle's moment of milky baby bliss is interrupted by the sharp trill of a message on her phone.

Lance.

I am going to Mum's 70th birthday party whether you like it or not.

Elle tenses. Considers her mum's desire. Replies.

How about you go in the morning, say 10-12, and I will go 1230-230? That way we can both celebrate with mum.

Send.

The reply comes quickly.

No. I will be there start to finish and you can get fucked if you think you can keep me away.

Elle scoffs. She was trying to accommodate them both. Trying to placate her own abuser. Putting her feelings towards her brother away and trying to compromise. Trying to put her feelings aside in order for her mother to enjoy her birthday party. Like all those years ago, here is Elle once again allowing other people's needs to be met before her own. Yet here is Lance, again showing her what an arsehole he is. *Fuck you, Lance,* she mouths. Elle decides not to respond to him and confidently deletes his messages.

Instead, she texts her mum.

Sorry mum, party is cancelled. Let's have a small lunch at a surprise venue instead.

Send.

Elle smiles down at Asher and tells him what a clever mother he has.

Bringing her baby up to her breast for his afternoon feed, she rocks in the armchair and sullenly remembers the last time Lance ever touched her in that uncomfortable way. She had returned from her travels through England and Europe and had found herself visiting her brother in Sydney. They met at a bar at the Rocks, a trendy tourist precinct with a historical charm of cobblestone footpaths covering its controversial colonisation past.

Lance had already had a few drinks. Elle could tell by the way his forehead was beaded with sweat and his voice was louder than usual. He stood a foot above the crowd and waved at her as she entered the busy pub.

"Hey!" he shouted at her.

Elle slunk into his powerful embrace, politely smiling at his friends sitting around the bar table.

"This is my little sis." He twirled her around and she obliged him with the performance. In hindsight, she cringes.

A few beers turn into a few vodkas and Elle is quite drunk. Lance is firing up for a night of clubbing, but Elle declines his persistent requests to join him. Annoyed, he pushes her in the arm and hisses, "Fuck off, then. Go home." Elle sways in the night air as Lance and two of his mates screech out to a taxi, flagging it down in a flurry of arms and cackles.

"Oi!" Elle calls out. "How do I get home? You can't leave me here."

"You lived in London, you tramp, you can find your way out of the city." And Lance slams closed the taxi door, red eyes disappearing into the sea of traffic.

Elle's head is foggy and she feels a pang of anxiety. She knows she is at the Rocks, and she knows she is staying at Lance's place at Artarmon, and she knows where the key is, but she is drunk and realises she doesn't have any money for transport. Being nineteen, drunk, and alone in the city is not her idea of fun.

She decides to call Katie.

Elle sits on the fence of someone's darkened duplex as she waits for her friend to pick her up. Katie arrives, obviously annoyed. Elle makes small talk and tries to hide her drunkenness. But trying to give Katie directions to find Lance's apartment proves challenging. A half-hour trip turns into an hour and fifteen minutes and Katie's lips are pursed tightly when she finally turns off the engine. It is after midnight.

"It's late, Elle. Reckon I can crash here tonight and I'll leave early in the morning?"

"For sure, you can stay."

They climb into the double bed in the spare room. It is not long before they are both fast asleep. If only their sleep was long, peaceful and uninterrupted. If only Lance did not arrive home in the early hours of the morning, high and horny. If only Elle did not lie like a statue as she felt him pull back the covers and nestle close behind her, stroking her leg. She lay with her eyes open in the dark, paralysed.

Katie stirs, opens her eyes and screams out, "What the fuck?"

Sitting upright now, her shadow block-art on the wall. A street light flickers outside. Elle hears Lance fumbling with his pants. She stays still, too scared to move. Her relief that Katie has woken is quickly sliced by her shame and embarrassment.

"I'm sorry; sometimes I sleep in here. Sorry, I didn't know you were here." Lance's voice is deep and controlled. He rolls out of bed and slinks out of the room.

Elle feels nauseous. The shame explodes like lava, frothing and scorching.

In the dark, Katie puts her hand on Elle's shoulder; Elle is still furled in the fetal position, her legs pulled up against her chest. Silent tears roll down her sticky cheek.

"Elle?" Katie rubs her arm now, leans closer, rests her head gently on Elle's pillow. Katie brings her fingertips to Elle's cheek and touches the tears sparkling in the eeriness.

In the stillness of the Devil's Hour, the two friends lie side by side. No more words are spoken, and the silence is deafening.

CHAPTER 31

James—Childhood Games—1990s

Growing up at Koolewong, James, Elle, and Lance have the run of the bush. Together with the other kids on their street—there are many—they build cubby houses out of palm fronds and play armies, digging trapdoors and burying food supplies. It's the mid-eighties and the only TV they watch are a few cartoons on Saturday morning. James is classed as a "little kid" and he acts that way. With his snow-white hair, squishy cheeks with a cheeky dimple, and blue eyes that crinkle into slits when he smiles, James draws people in wherever he goes. The kids who live next door, Katie and Sara, have warmly accepted him as their little brother as well. James has infiltrated their family with his wit and charm, to the extent that he claims the girls' grandparents are "my Nanny and Poppy". The girls laugh and wrap their arms around his little body, cooing and cheering. The two homes are separated only by overgrown grass and a wonky timber verandah. The kids climb between the two homes, racing up and down stairs, dressing up, jumping in the pool, darting down to the creek to catch frogs, and playing marbles in the dust bowl on the street corner. Other kids would join them in the escapades, the Hilliers-up-the-road, the Franks-across-the-road, and sometimes the Blanches-down-the-road. The parents are always somewhere, but the kids aren't too sure where, nor do they care. The Street and the Bush is their world and they are in charge. But there is an order to the hierarchy and James often finds himself at the bottom.

Lance's friend Jasper is visiting. Jasper lives further up the street in a house no-one ever visits. It is hidden up a long, steep, and curling driveway. Apparently, the other kids whisper, Jasper's mum was a "druggo" and left him when he was just a baby. Now Jasper's dad looks after him, but no-one ever sees the father. It seems so strange to all the other street kids. There are some families whose dads had left, but never a mum.

Lance and Jasper are the "big kids" and they are terrifying to the younger ones. At fifteen and fourteen respectively, Jasper and Lance loom metres above everyone else. Their hair is long at the back and short around the sides. Jasper has fur growing on his chin and Lance has an eyebrow ring. They wear dark T-shirts and ripped jeans. They talk differently, saying words like "rad" and "dude" and "fuck". Elle and James don't know what these words mean and they feign disinterest. They flick their marbles across the dust while Lance and Jasper smoke a cigarette.

"Oi, you," Jasper calls out to Elle. She pretends not to hear him and scampers after her cat's eye.

"Spazzy Ezzy," shouts Lance.

Elle looks up and scowls.

"Shut up!" She tries to sound braver than she feels. She suddenly wishes her mum was up on the verandah, calling to her to come in for lunch. Or she wishes her best friend and closest neighbour, Katie, hadn't gone to Little Athletics and that she was here with her now. Preschooler James ignores everyone and is playing with a stick, digging out another hole for the marble run.

* * *

It is later that day and Lance has locked himself in his bedroom downstairs. Pearl had part of the garage converted into another room when Lance turned eleven. He had outgrown the bunk bed he shared with Elle and had voiced his need for his "own space". Pearl noticed how her first born had grown tall and lanky, how he wanted to spend more time with his mates than with the family. She conceded and allowed a lock to be put on the door. But it is easily opened with a five-cent piece used in the slot to turn the latch. Lance put signs on his door that read *Keep Out!* and there is a faded Cure sticker as an homage to his favourite band.

Jasper has gone home and Lance is in his room. "Step By Step" by New Kids on the Block is playing on his tape player. A lava lamp glows in the corner on a wooden corner desk with a hutch, graffiti scratched into the yellow timber. There are damp towels on the floor and the unmade bed sulks under the window, curtains drawn, even though it is only 4 pm.

James bangs on Lance's door.

"Piss off," Lance shouts.

"Lance, I wanna come in."

Lance sighs, closes his *Hustler* magazine and lets in James, who is unaware of Lance's erection under a baggy T-shirt. The little boy jumps onto his big brother's bed, smiling. Lance stands over him, glances at the magazine lying next to him, feels the blood thumping in his penis. He reaches behind him and locks the door.

"Hey, little guy, wanna play that game we played last time?"

James's smile fades and he looks unsure.

"Do I have to go into the cupboard again?" James's eyes widen.

"Yes. Into the cupboard. And don't make a noise."

James starts to whimper but Lance picks him up and holds him close, whispering, "I will kill you if you make another peep, you little shit."

Upstairs, Elle is reading a book.

Across the road, Pearl is having a cup of tea with a neighbour.

CHAPTER 32

James—Lismore Hospital—2020

He is sitting in the lounge watching a show about zombies. Lily has gone out with her friends, which pisses him off. Since returning from Vietnam and having to stay in the hectic lockdown in the quarantine facilities in Sydney—*like they were fucking lepers*—the lust between him and Lily has faded. Lately, Lily is spending more time away from him and he doesn't know how to take it. She seems more distant, and James is terrified she'll leave him. Instead of talking to her about the way he's feeling, he drinks more frequently and then sends her nasty text messages until she comes home. But tonight, while he was shitty about her going out, he had a special patch in his pocket he couldn't wait to try. He checks the time: it was 7:28pm.

James and Lily's little beach side unit is sparsely decorated, but it's comfortable. The lounge is well worn and the TV on the wall is larger than the one in the bedroom. Scattered around the floor are items of clothes and discarded shoes, empty takeaway containers, and drink bottles. Neither Lily nor James cares too much for tidiness.

Since leaving the halfway house at Byron, James moved between a few units all promptly paid for by the Department of Veterans Affairs pension. James didn't mind Ocean Shores, and he had surfed every day with his new mates. He joined the local gym and trained every second day. From Ocean Shores, he had a stint at Pottsville with a guy whom he had met in the army. He didn't stay there for long, as there were many people coming and going and James felt as though he needed his own privacy.

Things had been going well with Lily. After dinner one night, when James was driving Lily home to her flat in Suffolk Park, he suggested that they move in together. Lily had looked at him, those deep blue eyes twinkling in the darkness. He remembers how she reached out, placed her hand on his thigh and squeezed tightly while leaning over to kiss his cheek. Of course she would move in with him.

At this stage, James was only drinking socially. It wasn't until after Lily moved in and they started arguing that the daily drinking routine crept back into James's sphere. She tried to draw his attention to it, which made James mad, and then he drank more.

Sitting in the lounge, zombies screeching from the telly, James presses pause on the remote. He pulls two small transdermal patches from his back pocket and rolls them around in his fingers, smiling. His mate, a guy he met through the meetings—*what a great guy*—told James about this drug coming out of the US.

"It's fucking wicked, man. Heaps better than oxy. Or benzos. I can get you a couple of patches from a guy who is a paramedic. Top shit." And James felt a rush of excitement course through his body. The adrenaline rush of doing something so fucking dangerous, he would be high enough to fly.

Now that Lily isn't home to challenge him, asking annoying questions about all the drugs he takes, he feels like he can breathe deeply. She is always pestering him, like she can control what he is putting in his body. Not tonight—tonight he is trying fentanyl.

He has already had a two-day supply of oxy and quite a few alcoholic drinks in the space of a few hours, so he is feeling sparkly and ready for the next surge. He unwraps one of the packets, and it reminds him of a nicotine patch he had to wear while he was flying long haul to the US. He peels off the backing paper, rubs his upper arm, and smooths the patch onto his skin, pushing and levelling it against his skin.

Ten minutes lapse and James isn't feeling anything different. Weird. The guy said it would be quick and it "would be a lot". He was hesitant about selling James two patches, as he said one would definitely be enough, and that it could last nearly twenty hours. James assured him he was going to give the other patch to his girlfriend, and the guy believed him.

Now, James unwraps the second patch and puts it on his other arm. Rubs and smooths. It hits him. Like a wave, he is smashed by a cool rush of euphoria through his entire body. Groggily, his head swims underwater and the TV drifts away from the lounge, flying up into the ceiling and zigzagging away, further and further. James lets out a girlish giggle and falls backwards, allowing a deep relaxation to overcome him.

Suddenly, there are all these people in the room. Cops, ambos maybe. Uniforms, bright lights. There's Lily, swimming into view, straddling him and crying, thumping his chest. Someone in a uniform is grabbing her and James wants to tell him to stop and to get his fucking hands off his girlfriend, but a thick, sticky sensation stops him from moving. What the fuck? James's dilated eyes inadvertently close again as he is swallowed by gnarly shadows.

When he awakes the second time, he thinks he is in an ambulance. Somewhere there are sirens blaring. *Turn them off*, he tries to say, but the words won't take shape. His mouth is dry and he can hardly keep his eyes open. James tries to lift his head, but can't. Lily is next to him, crying and squeezing his hand. But James is panicked that he can't feel her hand in his. Numbness has taken hold. Confused, he sinks back into the darkness of the coma.

CHAPTER 33

Elle—Hospital—2020

It is January 2020 and Elle has recently given birth to a squishy-faced, windmill-armed baby.

Pregnancy had given Elle a new insight into living in her body. She traded nightly wine for calming chamomile tea, and bedtime crime novels for stories of natural births written by an awe-inspiring midwife, Ina May Gaskin. As Elle's belly swelled, so did her self-confidence. Elle and Bryce decided they wanted a natural birth, without intervention. Filled with the knowledge of positive birthing stories, Elle sought to reclaim the strength and trust in her *yoni*. She decorated the house with positive birthing affirmations: *I am brave and capable; Each wave will bring me closer to my baby; I trust my choices.* Channelling the wisdom, bravery, and intuition of the women who had birthed for centuries before her, Elle felt the spirit of her mother, grandmother, and great-grandmother encouraging her to trust her feminine wisdom. It was about time Elle took control of her body. She did not know just how transformative growing and birthing a baby could be in the healing process of her trauma.

To ensure her body could withstand the marathon of labour, Elle swam laps each morning, feeling the bubble of her baby held lovingly and weightless in the water. In the afternoon, Elle would take to the yoga mat and stretch her widening hips and aching lower back, breathing deep into her womb, connecting with her child. She imagined the beginning of labour, and how she planned to make her way to the ocean and lie in the gentle waves. Ideally, she would breathe through each contraction and ride the waves in the sea.

As it happened, there was no time for being rocked in the gentle waves of the ocean during the tightening of her uterus. There was no time for lighting a candle and reciting the positive affirmations. There was no time for Bryce to massage her back and squeeze her hips. From the first contraction to the last, only thirty-one minutes passed.

It was not the plan to freebirth at home, but baby Asher had his own plan for entering the uncertain world. With wild, unprecedented bushfires setting most of the east coast of Australia alight that summer, Elle had spent the final two weeks of pregnancy in a state of impending evacuation, concern, and unease. The baby waited eleven days past his suggested due date before arriving in a fiery explosion of hurried urgency that Elle will forever remember as perfection.

Bryce missed it all. Luckily, Pearl was there to deliver the baby. She had arrived a few days earlier to stay with Elle in those final days of pregnancy and together they had swum, laughed, and cooked wholesome food to add to the chest freezer. Pearl shared her own birth stories, and Elle devoured every word, admiring the strength of her mother to have three natural births. Over dinner one night, Pearl told her daughter about her own mother, birthing six babies in eight years during the fifties. A time of poverty and no time-saving technology like dishwashers and washing machines. While speaking of her mother, Pearl's eyes glistened with tears and her far-away gaze made her look youthful. Elle watched her mother, smiling softly, reliving the years of being the eldest, yet still a child herself, washing cloth nappies in a tin bucket, feeding her younger brother bread soaked in egg yolk, and bathing with her sister Leslie in tepid water in a rusty bathtub outside. Pearl remembers the love her mother gave to all of her children, the warmth and bosom-safe hugs. These stories will live long through Elle, the stories of admiration and hardship. The stories of endurance and gentleness. Sitting in the kitchen, holding a warm cup of tea, listening to her mum speak of her childhood, Elle traced her swollen belly with light fingertips, circling the divine energy growing within.

When Elle feels her first contraction in the afternoon of a very hot day in December, it is Pearl who rubs her lower back and tells her to breathe slowly. Pearl suggests they go to the hospital, but Elle could already feel the baby's head emerging, and while crouched on the carpet in her bedroom, she already knew there was no way she could walk to the car. With the wisdom within, Pearl helped Elle deliver the baby safely, slimy and slippery onto the poo- and blood-stained bed. And not for a single moment in the intensity of the thirty-minute transcendence had Elle felt afraid. Her mother was there, holding the spirit of her own mother, and her mother's mother, and the strength of all of the women who have come before.

Elated, relieved and holding her baby son on her naked body, Elle cries. Pearl reaches out, strokes her face, kisses the baby on his head, and when she looks up again, her face is filled with pride.

* * *

Asher is now six weeks old, and Elle is finally emerging from her baby bliss bubble. Bryce and Elle told their friends and family that they would be staying inside for six weeks, alone with their new addition to the family, who conveniently appeared earthside shortly before Christmas. The days and nights rolled into one. Elle peels herself away from the memory of milk-soaked clothes, 2-am Netflix shows, consuming one-handed snacks, soaking her swollen vagina in warm salty water, and revelling in two-hour increments of sleep. Bryce is helpful. He cooks and cleans and sleeps in the spare room to give her and Asher space. There was an opening in their life, a wide gaping hole that has now been filled by a tiny human who needs everything from his parents just to stay alive. Elle is exhausted yet buoyed. She is grateful yet resentful.

It's an overcast summer's morning and Elle takes Asher for a walk in the baby carrier. She is healing and feels the need to stretch her legs and leave the confines of her darkened bedroom. The air is moist and dewy. She wanders slowly past her neighbours' homes, past the horses and the sheep grazing in the paddocks. Her baby squirms and coos, fighting sleep. Elle walks with a hand resting on Asher's lower back, curling him close to her as she did in the later stages of pregnancy, as though protecting him from the unseen shadows lurking in cupboards and under stairwells.

On her return from the slow walk, it is Bryce who meets them at the front gate. Elle notices how the passionfruit vine is reaching its tendrils out towards them, searching for a place to rest. Bryce opens the gate and puts his arm around her, kisses the top of her head.

"Your mum called while you were out."

There are bees hovering above the cosmos flowers and Asher reaches a fat little fist towards Elle's chin. She watches the bees, working hard to collect the pollen to take back to their queen. The females—they are the working bees—do all the work, foraging, pollinating. The male bees have only one job: to pleasure the queen.

Bryce takes a step towards her and the bees move to the next flower, the white star jasmine, Elle's favourite flower. Bryce's face is stretched with a concern Elle has not seen before. The furrow between his eyes deepens and his beard twitches next to where his lips should lie.

"It's about your brother."

But Elle already knew that.

* * *

A mere two hours later, Pearl is parking her white Mazda outside of Elle and Bryce's home. Elle meets her there, suitcase in one hand and Asher bundled in the other. Bryce holds the baby car seat, still with a furrowed brow top and clenched jaw. He fastens the seat into place, holds his son tightly, and whispers in his ear the truth of a father's love. Asher is strapped into the car seat, his tiny, balled-up body nestling between the cushions and the muslin cloth draped over his legs. Elle hugs Bryce, squeezes his large and warm body close to her, buries her head into his shoulder. The shoulder she has spent many nights sleeping against. The shoulder she has cried into when moments have been unforgiving and uncompromising. The shoulder she has watched hold their son, bobbing and rocking. Elle inhales Bryce's smell—damp earth, petrol, campfire smoke—and feels his breath on her cheek.

"I love you."

* * *

It's a six-hour drive to the hospital. Pearl and Elle talk about the small things and the big ones. They stop twice so Elle can feed the baby and change his nappy.

As they near the hospital, Elle asks again what the doctor said.

"I told you, Ez, he asked if I was Pearl, James's mum. I said yes. He said James was on life support. He said I should make my way to the hospital."

"That's it? Did he say how or what happened?" Elle is frustrated at her mother's lack of inquiry. Uncertainty is like wind to fire for Elle; she feels the heat rising within her. From the back seat, Asher cries and Elle ignores him.

"I didn't ask, Ez. I just felt so overwhelmed I started packing, called you, and just left straight away."

Even though Elle and Bryce had declared a baby bubble for six weeks, James had invited himself for Christmas and to that Elle could not say no. She had not seen her brother for months, hardly at all since he had fallen in love with Lily. The day before Christmas, James and Lily arrived and Elle took one look at him and her heart sank, the world tilting once more. James's eyes were dark and ringed by a grey pool of sleeplessness. Lily stood behind him, coy and cool, cotton slip dress draped effortlessly over her bony figure. James introduced Lily to his sister and then danced his way inside, scooping up Asher as Bryce put out a hand to steady them both. Bryce caught Elle's eye, and she knew he could see the disappointment, the heartache, the longing for things to be different this time.

Bryce and James made small talk before James handed back the baby and went to the fridge.

"Where's the beer?" he called.

"Outside in the garage, mate," said Bryce.

James found the cold beer and opened it, jeering at Lily and Elle. He could feel his sister's judgement, but he didn't give a fuck. It was Christmas.

* * *

The hospital is brick and tomb-like, with tiny windows as eyes peering out across the car park. There are ghosts, demons, angels, and saints all lingering around and within the building. It's nearly dinner time and Pearl and Elle are exhausted after the long drive. Elle bundles Asher into the baby carrier and he protests loudly.

Walking along the bleached corridors, Pearl takes the lead. Elle protectively wraps her arms around her baby. Her instincts are shouting at her to not be here, in this sick and morbid place, yet her heart is aching for her brother. Elle needs to be here. James needs her to be here.

They reach intensive care and find James's bed. They hear him before they see him. He is laughing. Pearl smiles and breathes a deep sigh of relief. Elle inhales sharply; Asher's cries are getting louder.

The small, white-curtained room looks small as James's bulky body dressed in black takes up most of the space, his thighs pressing on the edges of the bed and limbs draped in cables and sticky electrodes. He looks up from the cigarette he is rolling out of loose tobacco, surprised.

Pearl goes to him first, hugs her youngest son, and allows two small tears to spill from the corner of her eyes.

"What are you doing here? Why are you crying?" James speaks loudly, unsmiling.

Pearl explains that someone from the hospital had called her. James is mad at hearing that and says it's his business—*they don't have the right*. Pearl pats her eyes and squeezes James's hand, but he pulls away so he can continue rolling tight little tubes of tobacco.

Lily is perched on the end of the bed, cross-legged.

The doctor squeezes into the cramped space. There is a polite exchange between the members crowding the room before the doctor tells James he needs to stay under observation. James argues with the doctor, saying he just needs "to go home and get out of this fucking place".

"Fentanyl stays in your system, and we don't know how it will affect you. You need to stay under observation for at least twenty-four hours. While we have reversed the symptoms of the fentanyl, I highly recommend you stay."

"Fuck that. I only took a 50 mg patch, and when that didn't work, I put another on." James is dismissive. Lily curls her long legs in towards her chest.

"I understand you feel okay now and you imagine your body is okay, but you really don't know the seriousness of this situation. Your heart could stop again." The doctor steps closer to James, who scoffs rudely. "Think about Lily. If you go home now, like you want to, your heart could stop again at any time in the next ten hours or so. She has already done an amazing job of resuscitating you once—do you really want her to do that again?"

They all look at Lily.

Suddenly, James laughs and says, "It wasn't that bad. Come on! Look at her, she's fine."

Lily, face ashen, holds up her hands slowly. Pointedly. One wrist is swollen, and a light blue bruise in the shape of a heart has formed.

"James," she says softly. "It was really scary. Look at my hands. It hurt so much. Your lips were blue. It was actually really traumatic. You were dead." Tears fill her ocean eyes.

At this, James laughs loudly again. "Traumatic? Come on." He glares at her coldly. "Don't be dramatic."

Elle lingers by the curtains, swaying from side to side, trying to calm her tiny baby. She is suddenly very conscious of where she is: a hospital full of germs and viruses and bugs and sickness and death. During the long drive, she had imagined her brother in a coma, lying in the shadows between life and death, floating on the edge. Her thoughts had conjured the sight of a dying man, heartache and demons pulling him away from the cruel and unforgiving world where he could not run fast enough.

Yet here she saw a different sight. Here is her brother, rolling a cigarette, sitting up in bed like a prince, his beautiful girlfriend now stroking his feet. Where he should be grateful and remorseful, he is rude and dismissive. And Elle realises that a darkness has crept into his soul and is overtaking the gentle, funny, and charismatic boy he used to be.

Elle feels sick. She left the safety and warmth of her home and bed and lover, with a six-week-old baby, to drive six hours, to be by her dying brother's side. She did not think twice about bundling up her baby and barrelling up the highway to be with her brother with little information about the state he was in. Elle and Pearl did not, for a single moment, hesitate. They knew they needed to be there with James in his darkest hour.

The rage bubbles inside her, deep down in the depths of *her* darkness.

"Listen to the doctor, James. Listen to Lily. You need to stay here for the night. We can come back and get you tomorrow." This is the first time Elle has spoken. Asher is still grumbling. James flashes his eyes at her, a silent standoff.

The doctor, Pearl, and Lily all nod but nobody speaks, watching James for his response. Machines beep and flash. Outside the room, someone shouts and the sound of trundling metal over tiles echoes.

"Can't, sis," he says finally, flatly. "I can't stay here. I can't sleep here. All these lights and beeping and fucking noises."

Deep sigh.

"I'd rather be dead."

Sniff.

"Please let me go home."

CHAPTER 34

Elle—Farm—1996

Elle is twelve and her life has been uprooted.

With Eleanor and James in tow, Pearl follows Don to the farm on Biripi Country. After long arguments, Lance convinced her that he was old enough to stay at home alone. He is eighteen, after all, and has just flunked his final exams at school, but Pearl won't find out about that for a few more months. For now, she believes her eldest son is responsible, intelligent, and respectful. She agrees to let him stay, conditionally. The condition is that Lance pays board and the house stays tidy for the real estate inspection, as Pearl intends to sell it as soon as they are settled in their new farm life. Neither James nor Elle misses Lance being in their daily lives. But they don't articulate this to anyone.

The farm is idyllic and sweeps in a long peninsula between Camden Haven River and the tender curve of Watson Taylor Lake. The House that Don Built sits next to the train line, nestled under Middle Brother Mountain. It is a sprawling timber home with gaps between the frame and the walls, second-hand kitchen appliances, and individual stained-glass windows that Don has made during his down time over the years. He is good with his hands. A stained-glass black cockatoo framed by an orange setting sun glimmers above the TV cabinet in the lounge room. Above the front door, a pink-and-red banksia reflects the sun during the middle of the day. Don, whilst being a talented builder, fisherman, gardener, and hunter, has had very little experience with children, and most definitely none of his own. After seeing Pearl for the past three years, this is the longest he has been in a relationship with a woman who has children. Elle is nearly a teenager and she is highly sensitive and emotional. James is eight and full of energy and comic wit, eager to learn the skills of his step-dad. Don tries, pathetically at times, to be a role model.

The farm offers endless days of outdoor play. Elle has a horse and she spends days on end riding the buckskin gelding through the paddocks, singing out of tune to Tori Amos songs she remembers by heart. This is the mid-nineties, and Elle has only recently acquired a six-stacker CD player, long before the music devices become portable. Singing out of tune and repeating the chorus is the best she can do for now. And anyway, her horse doesn't seem to mind.

James longs for a motorbike, but he is too young, too reckless, too irresponsible to be trusted with one. So he rides his dirt bike down the long track between the swampy, mosquito-infested mangroves and down to the river bank. Here there is a caravan perched atop a hill, next to the water tank. Down by the river's edge, a clearing has been made by years of school holiday visits and tiny feet jumping, climbing, dripping, jumping again. To the right of the clearing, a rope swing has been lovingly tangled to the furthest, thickest branch of a mangrove. And underneath this rope swing bobs a rusty old tin dinghy. At the bottom of the dinghy, rolling around, are fishing hand reels, a broken net, and a pair of thongs.

Today, however, James is not by the river. He is at a friend's place having a sleepover.

Today, Elle is at the river, sitting on the bank in her swimmers, wet and muddy. Sitting next to her Lance.

This is the first time Lance has visited his family up north.

Lance hates the farm. He hates Don, too. He tells his mates the farm is *bogan-ville, red-necked, bum-fucktown*.

Lance lights a cigarette and asks his little sister if she would like one. "Um, no." She shakes her head. Lance notices the way her boobs are starting to form, tiny nubs pushing through the worn Lycra of her swimwear. He stares for a moment, then looks away.

He asks Elle about life up here.

"How's the school?"

"It's okay."

"Any friends?"

"A couple."

"What about boyfriends?"

She looks at him coldly, repulsed. "No!" she nearly shouts.

Lance laughs at her, his little sister who is growing up and trying to be firm with him. His laugh is cold and malicious. Condescending. Elle feels shame pulsing through her body.

Her older brother finally turns away and looks out at the river, leaning back on his hands. It's quiet. There is no-one around for at least two kilometres. He would hear anyone coming by car, and anyone coming by boat. And either way, travellers could not see the two of them, tucked away behind the caravan on the hill and between the shade of trees on the riverbank.

Elle is quiet, considering he has not seen her for a few months. He is slightly offended by her coyness. Lance thinks she needs to loosen up a little.

He reaches for his canvas knapsack, black graffiti and tiny circular badges haphazardly covering the material. He fiddles with the silver buckles and rustles out a brown paper bag. Noticing Elle has taken an interest, he quickly turns to her, a large smile on his face with those crooked teeth and big nose. She leans back slightly.

Lance holds out the paper bag.

"This is for you," he says.

"What is it?" she asks.

"Open it."

She does.

Inside, there is a small glass bottle filled with brown liquid. She reads the label: *Jim Beam*. Turning it over in muddy hands, she feels the coolness of the glass, the slickness of the neck. The shame seeps through her body again. She feels a desperate need to escape but her legs won't move.

"Drink it," he says.

And Elle always does as she is told.

CHAPTER 35

James—Nightclubs—2007

While Elle is getting ready to move overseas again, James has fucked up his living arrangements again. He was stupid enough to get caught gambling with the club's money, a scheme a mate told him was foolproof. Only it wasn't foolproof, because James kept losing, and before he knew it, he owed two thousand dollars that he simply did not have. Panicked, he told his manager, who angrily swore at him and then fired him. James's confidence was shattered. He kept fucking up, and he did not know how to get his shit together. Everyone around him seemed to be doing better than he was. His mates seemed to be holding jobs and settling down with lovers. James had been trying to meet up with Harley, his best mate from school, but Harley had excuse after excuse—work commitments or sport or some other bullshit. Now and then, James would send another text, but the delays in replies were longer and longer. Going through his contacts list, there were fewer and fewer people he could rely on to answer his call. Even when James spoke to his dad, there was a tone of annoyance and judgement that cut through the air. *If only he knew*, thought James bitterly. Feeling isolated, broke and pathetic, James started smoking more weed to numb the pain of the shame.

Earlier that year, when James just turned eighteen, it was his brother Lance who said, "Come hang out in the city." Hesitant at first, James did not know how to articulate the feelings of not being safe; instead he leant into the thrill of being in the city after his quiet existence in the sleepy beachside town where he spent his teenage years. Since Simon had rejected James's request to live with him, James was spending more time with his older brother.

"Sure," replied James. "I'll come this Saturday."

In his beat-up rusty white van, James chugs down the freeway and meets Lance at his apartment at Artarmon late Saturday afternoon. Lance, now in his late twenties, has been working as a computer guy at a large firm in Chatswood. He rents a small but well-positioned unit near the station at Artarmon, so it is an easy ride into the city. Lance always laughs loudly and is often playing practical jokes. James and Lance, by most accounts from the outside, get along and talk easily. After all, Lance is a role model to his younger brother. Lance knows stuff, and he was the first to introduce James to alcohol, porn, and soon, illicit drugs.

Tonight, in the city, will be the night James will swallow his first ecstasy pill, from the hand of his older brother. Being only eighteen, James is yet to recognise the signs of grooming. That will come later, when he is buried underground in the bunker of Tarin Kowt with all the time in the world to remember and analyse. Instead, when Lance holds a closed fist in front of James, a dorky, crooked-toothed smile leering at him, James, curious, asks what it is he is holding.

Lance turns his palm over and theatrically opens one finger at a time while James leans closer to see what magic Lance will reveal. Clustered in the middle of his palm are four red tablets moist with sweat. James feels the flutter of nervousness coupled with excitement as his adrenaline surges. James has heard of ecstasy—it was probably Lance who told him about it first—but he has yet to try any hard drugs other than the pot he regularly smokes. James is excited to escape the gnawing uneasiness he feels in the pit of his stomach whenever he is around his brother.

In the early 2000s, Lance was part of an underground rave scene where trance music, neon lights, and sucking on lollipops or baby dummies was the cool thing to do Thursday through Sunday night. There was a rise in methamphetamine availability and use, and Lance was one of those many young people who should have known better. He frequented the rages in dingy warehouses and seedy clubs across Sydney, staying awake for days. Afterwards, he would tell tales of adventures and mind-bending experiences to his impressionable little brother. James's eyes would light up at the craziness of the antics and he was bewildered by a scene so dramatically far from his weekends camping on isolated islands. James, tender, kind-hearted and naive James, was instantly mystified by the rave scene, and Lance preyed on this curiosity.

So here they are, Lance holding all of the power in his fist in the form of four tiny red pills with an imprint of an alien face stamped into the surface.

"Take two," Lance says and hands them over to his baby-faced brother.

James does as he is told.

James remembers the whole-body euphoria spreading like festive sparklers through his limbs. He allows his mind to float on a cloud of mystery, wonder, and awe as he sees the neon lights of the Harbour Bridge take shape. Out of the taxi and wafting along the pavement, James is led by his arm—tingling and weightless—down an alleyway by Lance. Lance, whose face seems transparent, his once-blue eyes now dark dinner dishes, laughs, blurs, and skips like an expectant child. James awkwardly stumbles along behind him, experiencing the buoyancy of every lunge.

James remembers lining up with an array of people waiting to get into a nightclub with flickering neon lights above the door.

He was trying to stop his body from dancing, swaying, gyrating. He remembers looking around and only seeing people smiling, eyes wide and skin sparkling like satin. Inside the club, the music pulsates through every cell, every strand of hair on his body standing upright, sensory overload. Lance puts a cold drink in his hand. James didn't realise how thirsty he was until the glass was empty. Head swaying, he swivels around looking for a table to place the glass, reaches, drops it, and laughs. Lance takes James by his hands and tugs him towards the dance floor. Sweaty, heaving bodies jump and sway and undulate. James falls into the sea of muscle shirts, shaved heads, and neon paint. The energy is captivating, and he rolls his body with the waves of sound, swept in the moment of no time, no meaning, no heaviness. He feels the arousal, deep in his stomach. Looking around at the silhouette heads, James realises there are only men. And the men are pulsing, pushing in around him. Somewhere, James hears a voice that is telling him to leave, but he is powerless against the rush of ecstasy that makes him forget what he just noticed. The cautious voice disappears into the thudding electro music. He sees his brother smiling, and James momentarily believes he is safe.

Soon, James is being pushed into a dark corner of the warehouse and is smothered by hands, a wet tongue, and a bony penis pushing. Pushing. James is saying *no*, but no-one can hear him over the music. That fucking music. *Doof, doof, doof.*

These are the harrowing demons that come back to haunt James for the remainder of his adult life. It takes many years for James to articulate the events of this night. The shame, the embarrassment, the naivety of his eighteen-year-old self. The hatred he holds inside, will, for many years to come, resurface, bubble and spill over the edges. The young man James was becomes stifled under the sticky shadow of Lance's opportunistic violence.

CHAPTER 36

Elle—Facing the Truth—2011

Years later, when Elle was in her late twenties, the intensity of the seven-year life-cycle struck her hard. The dramatic shift in energy altered her reality and she finally stepped into her own authority. By sinking low in a puddle of toxicity, she shed the oil and grime and confronted—*hard*—the reality of her childhood.

Her cousin was getting married and Elle had been invited to the engagement party. Ironically, it was a masquerade party in Sydney. Elle's anxiety was at its peak, and the night before the party, she had stayed up all night, her heart racing, feeling as though a steel hand was pushing firmly on her ribcage, heavy and suffocating. The more she tried to sleep, the more hyper-aware she became. Soon, the sun cracked over the horizon and the milky light filtered into her room. She dragged herself from bed, showered, and sullenly dressed for the big event.

Driving to meet her mum—as they were to travel to the party together—Elle's exhaustion made her hands shake and she could hear the blood circulating in electrical pulses in her brain. A cold sweat blanketed her skin. White knuckles on the steering wheel, fighting back the tears. More than once, she imagined careening off the highway into a tree, or worse—an oncoming car.

Elle visualised herself closing her eyes and yanking on the steering wheel. These dark thoughts clouded her mind.

Thankfully, Elle arrived at Pearl's home and staggered into the house, by now near hysterics. Pearl, shocked and confused, held her daughter tightly, allowing her to sob into her shoulder. Pearl remembered Elle as a three-year-old, sensitive and emotional. The small child would cling to Pearl's legs at every social event, shy and anxious. When Elle started school, each morning Pearl would heartbreakingly physically hand her over to the bus driver or the teacher or an older student, just so Elle would release the vice grip around Pearl's neck.

Today, Pearl was neatly dressed in a sky-blue skirt and a crisp white blouse, adorned with a gold necklace and hoop earrings. As her daughter choked and sobbed, Pearl was concerned about possible snot staining her shoulder and mentally waded through her closet, wondering which alternative blouse would be suitable for her skirt, as it was a truly beautiful skirt and really made her eyes stand out. Chasing away the thoughts, Pearl rubbed the back of her daughter's head and made shushing sounds, just like she had many times before. All this time, Pearl did not know what truly troubled her middle child. Elle had always been so introverted and secretive, especially as a teenager. Pearl recalls the dramatic poetry Elle wrote over the walls in her bedroom. The little notes she would leave under Pearl's pillow, cryptic collections of quotes and drawings. Once, when Pearl was cleaning Elle's room, she found a sketchbook of cartoon faces with dates and feelings written under each one. They were beautiful pictures, despite having tormented, obscure facial expressions, and words like *compunctious*, *alexithymia,* and *remissed* scrawled under each image. Running her fingers over the charcoal outlines and the careful shading, Pearl smiled sadly before tucking the sketchbook back into the drawer of Elle's desk. Something about the pictures troubled her, but she could not identify what the feelings were.

Now, twenty years later, Elle inhales deeply and pulls herself out of her mum's bosom, eyes red and puffy. Pearl notices that her daughter has the same childish look of discontent and stress, pursed lips and ruddy skin. Pearl takes Elle's hands warmly, looks her right in her eyes, and asks her, "What's the matter?"

And for the first time, Elle opens her mouth and tells her mother everything. Words fall from her soul, cascading like acid rain that burns and scalds. Pearl's face turns grey. The day turns into afternoon and the wind howls from the lake, blowing a stench of rotten seaweed through the home. After the stories of Elle's sordid memories and the ways in which her mental health and intimate relationships have been affected over the years, darkness has arrived.

Pearl pours two glasses of wine.

Pearl's initial response is denial. "Surely not? How could he have? Where was I?" Elle is too tired to respond and meekly shrugs her shoulders.

Her mother's second response downplays the seriousness of the abuse. "He was just a boy, I'm sure he didn't mean anything by it." At this, Elle bristles. Narrows her eyes and crosses her arms.

"No, Mum. The last time it happened, I was eighteen. That made Lance twenty-four. He knew better. He was not a bloody kid."

Pearl sips her wine, tears pooling in her eyes again; considers her daughter's words.

And, almost apologetically, she whispers.

"Unfortunately, this is what men do." She looks down at her hands. Her voice is hollow. "But as women, we overcome it. We are strong."

Even though Pearl is in her sixties, at this moment, Elle sees her as a young woman who birthed her so many years ago. She sees the woman who miscarried three babies before Elle was born. Who bled for days alone in the house while her husband worked, oblivious to her distress. Elle sees the teenager who helped raise her younger siblings while her own mother drank herself into a grave. Elle sees a young woman who has endured poverty, loss, and raising children on her own. She feels the warmth, the strength, the compassion radiating from her mother's aura. And it makes her feel conflicted. Elle loves her mother with every inch of her soul. She wants to be just like Pearl, forgiving and calm. Yet Elle does not feel strong. She feels lighter, to an extent. She feels the burden shared. But she doesn't feel the strength her mother speaks of right now.

Pearl's fourth response is to encourage Elle to talk with Lance.

"You need to talk with him and work it out."

Elle nods in all the right places and wipes her cheeks. She smooths her dress, tucks strands of hair behind her ear. Pearl hands Elle the phone and requests that she call Lance now.

Shaking and summoning the courage her mother speaks of, Elle presses the green button and listens to the echoing ringtone, thumping in her ear.

"Hello." It's Lance. His voice is hoarse and scratchy, as though he has just awakened from sleep.

"Lance, I've told Mum everything."

* * *

Elle and Lance go to a counselling session facilitated by a gentle, middle-aged woman, Janelle. Elle had been seeing Janelle for the better part of a year. When Elle had her first session, Janelle had been sitting in the black chair pressed against a blue wall, a window to her left with yellowing lace curtains. In the middle of the room was a coffee table topped with a notepad, a magazine called *Better Homes and Gardens*, and a box of tissues. Janelle had seen three clients that day. She was hungry and her lukewarm tea needed more sugar, but she sat calmly in her black chair and greeted Elle with a dutiful smile. Elle sat awkwardly across from her, crossing her legs, curly blonde hair swept up in a bun. At first impressions, Janelle saw an anxious young woman who was too skinny for her height, dressed conservatively in black pants and a floral blouse, and who smiled with her mouth but not with her eyes. Janelle noted how polite Elle seemed, like she was playing a role and had carefully scripted her words. Contained. Yes, contained and tense. Was that an oxymoron?

After making small talk, Janelle found out that Elle was a high school teacher, that she had lived there for a year and a half, and that she was very unhappy in her relationship. Yet this wasn't the problem, Janelle knew. There was more that Elle wanted to say.

Janelle asked her, "What brings you here today, Elle?"

Elle glanced out the window, stretched her fingers and clenched them again, twisting her thumb around her little fingers and feeling the tension in her ligaments. Janelle sat quietly, watching the movements of this young lady.

"I'm not doing so well, actually. It's that … well … my brother, he …"

Janelle shifted slightly to the left, crossed her legs, and knitted her eyebrows together, waiting.

Elle's eyes welled with tears and she let out a heaving sob as she said the rest. Once the first tear fell, a thousand more followed, and Elle was sobbing hysterically in the corner of the room, red-faced and blotchy, snatching tissues, one, two, three, wiping and blowing and stuttering. Elle cried for a solid ten minutes. Janelle watched her and nodded empathetically. She let the girl cry, and cry and cry, the floodgates opening a sea of emotions and years of silence. Janelle made a note on the paper in her lap. As an afterthought, she crossed out the word "contained".

Afterwards, when Elle had slowed her breathing and wiped her eyes again, inhaled sharply and consciously collected her body and mind, coming back into the moment, Janelle spoke.

"Elle, we will need to book at least six sessions together." And Elle nodded.

Six sessions turned into eight sessions, and it was the eighth session when Elle asked Janelle if she would counsel Lance and her. Janelle agreed, and Elle squirmed, wishing she had never asked because then she couldn't back out.

* * *

The following week, Lance catches a bus to Minimbah and checks himself into a motel.

Elle is at a coffee shop with her friend when she sees him walk past. Her heart stops. He notices her, waves, approaches. Elle fumbles with her chai and her friend stops speaking.

Lance says, "Hi. It was a long trip."

"Yeah," Elle agrees but offers nothing more.

The air is thick. Elle scratches at her neck.

Lance taps the table with his knuckles, looks away from her, down the street and says, "Rightio. I'll see you tomorrow?" Elle nods and lifts her hand in a half-wave. Then she turns back to her friend, who looks puzzled. Elle does not share any further information about the interaction, dismisses the questions, and returns to the teacher talk about the new curriculum and "how on earth are we going to write three new programmes before next term?"

* * *

On the drive home to her forest house by the lake, Elle cries. When she arrives in the kitchen, she cuddles Raff and sobs into his brown fur. He licks her face. She pulls herself up off the floor and pours herself a glass of red wine. It will be the first of many tonight and in the nights to come.

The next day, Elle dresses herself conservatively in light blue jeans and a long-sleeved black shirt. She pulls her hair up off her face and kicks on her Converse sneakers. Hugging her dog goodbye, she makes the drive into Minimbah and parks outside of the health centre in time for her appointment with Janelle and Lance. Skin sticky with sweat, her heart pounds and already she can feel the sting of tears piercing her eyes. She wishes her stress would show itself in other ways. Words of venom? Outrage where she can throw something or scream? Marathon-running? Instead, she just cries. Her face becomes red; her bottom lip quivers; her eyes well; her words are stifled. It's her body's default response whenever she is in a prickly situation and she always feels like a helpless child.

Sitting in Janelle's office on the couch where she has sat numerous times before, Elle clutches a handful of tissues. Grossly, Lance is perched, cross-legged, opposite her. To his right is Janelle, her glasses resting on the tip of her nose and a cup of tea in her hand. She smiles kindly at Elle and welcomes Lance to the meeting, saying something about how good it is he is here to bring clarity to Elle's memories.

The rest of the meeting is a blur of emotional upheaval and tidal waves of tears. Elle remembers telling Lance how hurt she felt about how he treated her as a child. The cupboard, the nights Pearl was playing tennis, the porn magazines he gave her when she was nine. Indignantly, Lance looks at her with bulging blue eyes and that gigantic, crooked nose, and he opens his arms and surrenders. Well, Elle stupidly expects him to surrender.

Instead, he says, "Those memories are actually mine. I was the one who was abused by a neighbour, and you must have heard me talking about it with Mum. But, Elle, I would never do that to you."

Janelle points her chin at Elle, whose mouth is agape and she can't quite find any words to come out, only strange little gasping noises of disbelief.

Lance sees his target as disarmed and he continues firing.

"You've been going through a lot, and your anxiety is really bad at the moment. It really sucks what you have been through, what with Mum moving and your shitty relationship."

Elle holds her breath and waits for the apology. Waiting for the acknowledgement. Waiting for remorse.

Lance continues. "But what you said happened—it simply didn't. I'm sure you've manifested these memories based on what I've been through. I don't blame you–you're very empathetic and you've always been really creative. I'm sorry you have been confused. Know that I never ever touched you."

Elle shakes her head and cries some more. She wants to scream at him, to throw something, to rip his blue eyes and his big nose off his face. Instead, she cries like a fucking baby.

Janelle lets her weep and passes more tissues. The counsellor leans on her elbows, checking the time.

Janelle starts to speak, with a rehearsed calm and reassuring tone.

"Elle, you know, I have been a counsellor for a long time. In my experience, it is very possible for a young person to make up stories, and this is called confabulation. Time has a funny way of altering perspectives and memories. Maybe, as children, as children do, there was a moment of exploration between you and Lance, and over time, this moment has altered into something much bigger and worse than the actual event. The fact that Lance is here today shows that maybe your perception of the event is a bit different to reality, and your perceived trauma is heightened at the moment due to your anxiety." She pauses and nods like her head is a full stop.

Elle wipes her eyes, rubs her neck, looks out the window. Sniffs again. Where are her fucking words?

Lance nods in agreement with Janelle. Elle spots a twinkle in his eye.

Janelle continues. "Elle, you say you have diaries of poetry and drawings. You told me these are full of memories. I think it is time you read over these and decide which are real and which are childhood imaginings, or else it is time to throw the diaries away and move on from these feelings of being a victim of abuse. As we have talked about, it is not serving you. There is peace in accepting and moving forward."

Feeling the shame engulf her like a flame swallowing a leaf fluttering in the wind, Elle nods. She inclines her head, politely thanks Janelle for her time. She makes little eye contact with Lance, who is leaning back in his seat now, legs uncrossed and a shadow of a smile on his face.

Elle stands, smooths her top, and leaves the room.

In her car, she cries like a small fucking child. A child who is locked in the cupboard and can't escape.

It is here, in the confinement of her car, that she promises herself something invaluable. She makes her inner child a promise, a "cross your heart and hope to die" kind of promise.

Looking at her swollen face in the rearview mirror, Elle swears that never again will she pretend that Lance is not her demon.

CHAPTER 37

James—Facing the Truth—2021

The problem with trauma is that the body never really forgets. James's body is beaten, whipped, and scarred. He flogs himself at the gym, pushing harder, screaming louder, growing larger. Thrashing his body, he hates all the mistakes he has made, all of the regrets and all of the shame. He is addicted to building his muscle size, knowing that no-one will come at him when he is built like a brick shithouse.

Although, in the true contradictory nature of addiction and trauma, in moments of clarity, James is pleased with how far he has come and the adversity he has faced. He is proud of his time in the army and how he served his country and often talks openly about his experiences. Willingly, he reveals the scar on his shoulder like a tattoo—a symbol of the pain he has endured.

Without the routine of the military, and without the financial freedom to travel like he did with Lily, it is easy for James to turn to drinking and misusing his prescription meds to create a sense of enjoyment.

Since Elle and Pearl helped him return home from his failed attempt at walking the Appalachian Trail when he was stranded in Washington (how embarrassing!), James has been in and out of rehab again. His relapse on the Trail lasted a while because weed is now legal in the States, and James had to bunker down with a relative until his new passport was issued. The weed helped him to pass the time and to ease his anxiety of being stranded in another country—again. What a fuck-up.

* * *

Sitting in a strange house with someone he hardly knew other than a Facebook profile, James thinks back to how he ended up here. James remembers being on the Appalachian Trail and how his legs were hurting after just a few days. The scenery was beautiful, but he was having a hard time staying present to appreciate the outlook. With a backpack full of his favourite pills, he admits to himself that he was swallowing more than he should have been. He recalls being high with a group of hikers and someone suggesting they drive to town. James was disoriented and confused in the morning, being half-dressed and shoeless outside of a busy train station. Maybe he was losing it—as he does sometimes—and the people who were driving the car dropped him off? He remembers being taken to hospital, scared and coming down like a sack of shit. And more than all of that, he angrily remembers the ridiculous fucking medical bills he had to pay. His bank account took a hit, and not having his bank cards to pay for it, he was properly screwed. Luckily, someone at the hospital contacted the emergency contact on the inside of his duffel bag and was able to reach a lady in Maryland who claimed to be his aunt. Ending up in the safe space of her home, James slept off his embarrassment and hangover during the space of a week.

James wanted his medication sorted as a high priority. The panic attacks were coming hard and fast, head spinning and heart palpating. It was when a neighbour offered him a joint that he realised he could legally stave off the clutching talons of anxiety. Meanwhile, trying to get his prescription meds back in order, as well as his passport re-issued, James needed to rely on his mum and sister, on the other side of the world in Australia, to help with the phone calls and paper trail, not knowing the full extent of how many hours Elle spent on the phone to the consulate—firstly, trying to locate him; secondly, trying to acquire an emergency visa; and thirdly, organising to have him medically evacuated. No, James did not know the half of it, but he knew he was furious that it was taking so fucking long to get home and out of the strange but compassionate aunt's house where he felt trapped. He needed his own phone, free internet, access to his contacts. Elle seemed to be fucking around and not doing much to help, even though he kept calling her and screaming about how important it was for him to fly back to Sydney. He needed help—couldn't she see that? And Lily, well, Lily was an emotional and sympathetic sounding board but she had no means to get him out of the country.

Finally, after three months of waiting for a new passport, James flew home to Sydney. His sister did not meet him at the airport—something about her kid Asher not being able to travel—and his mum wasn't waiting in the arrivals lounge, either. But Lily, the lovely, beautiful and forgiving Lily, greeted him with a warm embrace. No longer in an official relationship, her fondness for James and James's love for her allowed the fateful lovers to remain friends. As one of his only friends—where did they all go?—Lily agreed to help him sort his mess out again. From the airport to a hotel, she helped him check into a rehab in Western Sydney, Dharag Country. James would stay there for two weeks while Dr Wilson corrected his medication and he obliged her by attending the group therapy, albeit nonchalantly.

* * *

When James finally speaks with Elle on the phone, she is distant and vague. He tries to thank her for helping, but the shame stops the words from coming out as they should. Elle then reminds him of how "this is the second time I have bailed you out of a fucking country." Followed by, "Grow up, James. Get your shit together."

None of this advice helps James's already deflated self-esteem and the puddle of addiction he finds himself in. He reflects on the time in Vietnam, at the beginning of the money-spending spree, when Lily and James had the world at their feet and their love was unbreakable. He remembers riding on a moped along the winding roads, Lily's thin arms wrapped around his waist. He can still smell her hair and the coconut oil on her skin. The freedom they enjoyed together. There was no sense of time, no responsibilities. Just the two of them, travelling the country, sleeping in beautiful bungalows and exploring the captivating nature of sea and jungle. James was managing his anxiety well, drinking only enough to give him a buzz. He thought it was under control. Enveloping him like a sombre cloak of regret and remorse, James kicks at the ground and feels the tears sting his eyes as he remembers the last few sordid weeks in Vietnam.

When COVID hit—*so much hysteria*—Lily wanted to leave Vietnam. She was adamant that their travels had to hit pause, so James started looking for flights home. Unfortunately, the world had spiralled into chaos and lockdowns—whole airlines ceased flying and James could not find any flights out of Vietnam and into Sydney. He began to realise the seriousness of the situation when the once-friendly Vietnamese locals who had been serving them drinks and delicious meals at their venues now slammed the door in their faces and yelled at the white couple to "go back home!" James was shocked at the rudeness, and for a slight moment in time, he realised how foreigners in Australia felt when bogans brandished shirts and stickers that said *Go back to where you came from.*

Creeping back to the hotel, he admitted to Lily that he was wrong to want to stay, and now he couldn't even buy a bottle of water because the Vietnamese were terrified that he had COVID, despite the fact that he had been living there for months, and suddenly his tourist dollars did not count.

James called Elle to help.

"Please, sis, I can't seem to get a flight. Can you please help? I'll send you the money. Just please get us home."

Elle, while sounding despondent and conveying a concerning amount of heavy sighs, agreed to "look into it" and see what she could do.

Two days of thirst and hunger passed, with Lily and James hardly speaking to each other, before Elle called with an expensive but workable plan. They would catch a bus from Hanoi to Ho Chi Minh City, and there they would fly to Doha. The round trip would cost James just over twenty thousand Australian dollars. Checking his bank account, he calculated that it would leave him with six thousand dollars remaining. Shit. How did he spend that much money? Not to worry; he couldn't consider that at the moment. James and Lily needed to get on those planes and land back on home soil, where they could drink the tap water and be treated like first-class citizens again.

The trip home was long and tedious. James had a pocket full of Valium that he had bought in bulk in Vietnam shortly before lockdown. On the plane, mixing seven Vals with a couple of beers allowed him to relax into the journey somewhat. He was concerned as to why Lily was being so cold towards him. He had given her the window seat—which, of course, is the sign of deepest respect—and yet she stared out at the clouds in silence. A few times James had reached for her hand and leant over to kiss her cheek, but Lily shrank from his touch and meekly smiled as though to placate him. His love for Lily was intense and real and extraordinary. Together, they would conquer all. Yet here they were, strangers sitting next to each other. James forlornly tried to apologise for how he'd acted when he was high—how?—but his lack of clarity made it difficult. The Valiums made his head float and bounce and the thoughts were difficult to catch. Acknowledging how he had yelled at her a few times while he was drunk didn't seem to correct their course, and Lily hardly looked him in the eye the whole bloody trip back to Sydney. Eventually, after fruitless attempts to win back her affection, James's pining for forgiveness morphed into annoyance. When she still did not hold his hand or smile his way, the annoyance festered into anger. All he could truly find to be angry at her was the fact that he had spent so much money on her. How dare she now give him the cold shoulder!

After two days of travel, the pair arrived in Sydney, clad with thin surgical masks and having to *socially distance* from other people. Quarantine was intense and they were asked a thousand questions before being shepherded onto a people-mover van and taken to a looming brick hotel in Ultimo. Disembarking, names were read aloud and they were cordoned into small packs. Funnelling the groups away, a security guard took them up three flights of stairs and motioned to a room, number 305, telling them that was where they would stay.

Bravado and instinct made James step in front of Lily and open the door with the key left in the lock. Inside, noticing there were no windows that opened, straight away James felt the tension rise inside him. How could he smoke or vape without a verandah or a window to open? The walls of the room were squeezed, with a king-sized bed taking up most of the floor space, two small bedside tables, a tiny kitchenette with a microwave and kettle, and lastly, a poky, dark and musty bathroom.

This was where James and Lily were forced to spend two long, airless weeks. Confined, exhausted, tense. And every three days, someone, unidentifiable because they were cloaked in a disposable white suit and a useless mask, would knock on the door, leaving a RAT kit on the ground. The quarantined travellers locked inside had to complete the test to prove they didn't have COVID.

To pass the time, James used an online delivery service to have endless amounts of liquor and takeaway sent to their room. So much so, that on the tenth day of their fourteenth-day segregation, a guard came up to the room and told James he had had enough alcohol. James flew into an angry rage—"Who the fuck do you think you are telling me how much I can or cannot drink?"—until the guard slunk away.

Lily was quiet during their quarantine. Some mornings she would tell James about her dreams the night before, and together they would do a short workout of push-ups and squats, but mostly James was too unwell and hungover to do much with her. Lily lay on the bed, dozing in and out of sleep, trying to ignore James's angry rants. As he became drunker, he became angrier. James tried to explain to Lily how unfair it was to be locked away like this; how the people of Australia owed him more than this! After all, he'd served in fucking Afghanistan! James's verbal tirade turned to Lance and Simon. Why wouldn't Lily listen to him? He shook her shoulders. She groaned and shrugged his hand away.

Mournfully, James was beginning to realise that Lily would break up with him—for real, this time. Instead of talking this through with Lily, James drank more, yelled more, sulked more.

A deep ripping sensation inside his guts screamed regret.

CHAPTER 38

Elle—Healing—2025

As Pearl and Elle embark on another long-haul car trip north, the confines of the car become a sanctuary for mother and daughter. The familiar tunes of childhood songs fill the air—a playlist Elle thoughtfully curated—evoking a flood of cherished memories and shared experiences. With each Dolly Parton or John Williamson melody, Elle and Pearl's crackly, off-key voices intertwine in harmonious nostalgia, transporting them back to a time of innocence and joy. Outside the car, the landscape next to the highway turns from forests of ghostly eucalyptus trees into luminescent sugar cane fields, and their conversations flow effortlessly. Between singing, they reminisce over the birth of Asher, the adventure-filled camping trips from years ago, the idiocy of strange characters from their past, fond memories of Leslie, sharing silly and intimate stories about their friends.

They are on their way to Queensland, the Sunshine Coast. When James returned home from Vietnam, he was distressed, distant, and dishevelled. Lily broke up with him and Elle watched from afar as James spiralled downward into hardcore addiction and self-loathing. She tried a few times to suggest he re-enter rehab treatment, but he would assure Elle he was doing fine and did not need to be locked away. It wasn't long after this conversation that James called to say his therapist thought it was a great idea for him to walk the Appalachian Trail. Elle rolled her eyes as he spoke of faraway hillsides and healing under a starry sky. While she did not agree it was the best thing, she remained hopeful that the trip would cure his self-destruction.

James lasted four days on the trail before losing his sanity once again. Eighteen months have passed since James returned from the aborted hike. During this time, he had a few failed attempts at rehab in the short-stay centres in the city. Recently, when James confessed to Elle that he could buy drugs in the car park, Elle snorted at the irony. Saddened for her little brother, she could feel herself being less inclined to help him. Ripples of judgement clouded each conversation and then the conversations were few and far between.

Poor James, thought Elle. The waves of sobriety were small, and the tsunami of self-loathing was sinking him again. Eventually, it was Pearl who convinced him to commit to the long rehab programme outside of Brisbane, on Gubbi Gubbi country. She helped him with the application, chasing doctors' reports and liaising with his DVA case manager. Pearl, now snowy-haired and her wrinkles showing where her smile had been, was thankful for the financial support from the DVA. The treatment was thousands and thousands of dollars, which neither Pearl nor James had to spare.

Elle watched from a distance, not offering for James to stay with her nor making any phone calls on James's behalf—this time. She was wounded by his lack of gratitude for all the trouble trying to evacuate him from Washington. She was angry and resentful at how he had treated Lily while they were in Vietnam. She believed he had forgotten all the help she had offered over the past ten years, and she was mad. But mostly, Elle was holding onto the grief she felt for the little brother who was no longer there.

Elle, with her self-righteous nature, threw judgement on her brother's relapses. *Get better!* she groaned. *Just don't drink!* she lectured. All of these words meant nothing to James. He would stay sober for a few weeks then turn to the bottle again, and Elle was fed up. Now she had Asher and Bryce and her peaceful life in the country, she did not want any more of James's drama and negativity in her sphere. When she explained this to Pearl and gave her a prayer book about holding boundaries, her eyes welled and the simmering pain rose to the surface again. Pearl encouraged Elle to focus on her family. In the depths of the night, Elle felt terrible that Pearl was the only one now standing in James's corner. Guilty that her aging mother still held the intense stress of picking up the pieces of her adult son's fractured life. But Elle recognised that the strength of her mother's love was also her biggest weakness.

Once Pearl had secured for James the safety net of a three-month stay at the Queensland private facility, Pearl breathed a sigh of relief. Standing on the driveway with his duffel bag, Pearl watched as James was picked up by a DVA-funded taxi and chaperoned all the way to the Sunshine State. Pearl set to work tidying her house. She dragged armfuls of glass bottles from hidden spaces under James's bed and tucked inside shoe boxes. Swatted at her tears as she carried them to the recycling bin.

For the first few weeks of James's second attempt at long-term rehabilitation, neither Pearl nor Elle had any contact with James. The silence was reassuring, as it meant that James was safe and secure. Pearl's blood pressure began to drop as her sleep became deeper and more regular. She returned to her routine of beach walking, coffee with her girlfriends, and playing lawn bowls. Most of the conversations were around family, and Pearl spent many moments wishing for peace for her son. When she phoned Elle, they spoke about the positives of James being in a programme and how they both longed for the James they knew and loved dearly to re-emerge from the suffocating cocoon of addiction and self-destruction.

Soon James was given privileges, and one of the privileges was twenty minutes of a supervised phone call on a Sunday afternoon. Diligently, James called his mum every Sunday. He recounted the wins of his therapy, the skills he was learning, and his hopes for the future. And sometimes he called Elle when she wasn't busy with the toddler. As Elle heard how well James was doing and the clarity in his voice, she desperately wanted to believe him.

To believe is to see. And to see, Pearl and Elle organised a weekend to visit sunny Queensland.

They arrive at the clinic at nightfall. The tall trees surrounding the timber lodges wave in the shadows. A young man sees Pearl and Elle moving towards the administration office, and he jumps out of his seat, shouting James's name excitedly. James rushes from an adjoining room, arms thick with muscle and a whiteness to his eyes that Elle can see from metres away. Sparkling eyes. The last time she saw him, his eyes were red-rimmed, shadowy, puffy circles.

Now, he reaches Elle and Pearl and the three of them embrace.

"You look well, kiddo." Pearl smiles.

"Thanks, ma. I feel well."

Pearl signs the waiver to allow James to exit the centre for two nights. He is tiptoeing with elation, eager to leave, if only for a few days. Elle has booked them into a beach shack at Mooloolaba, within walking distance of the white-sanded beach. It's been too long between salty immersions.

Arriving at the small, rented home, the three of them choose their rooms. Pearl takes the largest, Elle chooses the bunk beds, and James opts for the lounge so he can fall asleep in front of the television. He tells Elle how much he has missed mindless streaming. In the clinic, he is restricted to watching inspirational YouTube lectures about the science of addiction and the true stories of those people who have conquered the suffocating grip of dependency. Tonight, after dinner, James will tune in to an action film and eat corn chips.

At dusk, Pearl, James, and Elle make their way to a local Mexican restaurant. It is balmy here in Queensland, where the humidity hangs in the air. They walk through a park that curls around a man-made dam. In the middle floats a small island surrounded by black swans and brown ducks paddling through the algae and lily pads. Overhead, bats begin to cry out, emerging from their resting place amongst the reaching arms of the fig trees. The sky is turning from orange to crimson to navy blue. The trio reach the restaurant as the street lights flicker on.

"What do you feel like?" asks Pearl as she scans the menu. Around her, laughing, smiling people are dressed up in cocktail dresses, false eyelashes, and plumped lips. The beachside restaurant is noisy and vibrant with young people enjoying their Saturday evening. Fairy lights twinkle around exposed timber beams and posters of Frida crinkle at the corners. A table next to theirs erupts in clapping and cheers. Someone is downing a pint of beer.

A waitress leans against Elle's side of the table, tapping an iPad.

"What can I get yas to drink?"

"Um, I'll have a soda and lime, thanks." Elle looks up at the waitress, who flicks her long ponytail over her shoulder.

James is still perusing the menu.

"I'll have a virgin margie," Pearl says with a nod.

Pearl and Elle watch James. His head is down, shoulders hunched. He runs his index finger over the text of the menu. Scans, pauses, sighs.

"I'll have this one." He points at the print, holding the menu up to the waitress's face.

"Number sixteen? Sure thing." She taps the screen and assures them she will be back in a few minutes to take their food order.

Elle feels an old twisting in her stomach. A squirming sensation that is a mixture of angst and concern. James is looking around the room now. He is clenching and unclenching his fists. Elle thinks, *This was a bad idea*. What was she thinking? Bringing a recovering addict to a festive Saturday night restaurant surrounded by pretty party people sipping cocktails. *Fuck*.

Pearl breaks the silence. "Oh, a juice!"

Elle is confused. Pearl is looking at the menu, smiling.

"Yeah. What did you think I was ordering?" James leans back in his chair. Scratches his beard.

Elle looks at the menu. Number sixteen. Orange, lime, pineapple, and mint. A fucking juice. Relieved, she laughs. James looks at her quizzically.

"Elle, did you think I'd ordered a cocktail?" He watches her closely. Elle stops laughing and glances at Pearl for support.

"Sorry James. Maybe this wasn't a great idea—coming here. We can go home if you like, play Taboo?"

James pushes his chair forward, fills his cup with water from a green glass bottle from the centre of the table. The shadows dance across his face. He narrows his eyes. Sips his water. Elle stiffens, clutches her handbag.

"You know, when I look at those chicks over there at the table, you know what I think about?"

Elle isn't sure she wants to hear the answer.

"I think that I was never like that. I was never like those girls—or those guys over there—going out on a Saturday night for a few drinks with friends." He takes another sip. Elle sits quietly and lets his words permeate her soul. He has not spoken honestly with her for so long, and she wants him to keep talking.

"A few drinks was never enough. I would have been on to my third drink by now, even though we've just sat down, and I'd be thinking about how I could get my fourth while everyone else was still on their first. I wouldn't have been listening to the conversation. I would have been itching to get to the bar, sneak a few shots of vodka while no-one was watching. I was never able to just sit and enjoy one or two drinks with my friends. Maybe that's why my friends have all left." James twists his fingers together. His eyes are glistening.

Elle steals a glance at her mum, whose eyes are also glinting in the light.

"I want to stay, Elle. I want to have fruit juice with my dinner, and I want to sit here and talk with you guys. I want to wake up sober tomorrow, and every day afterwards."

And he does. They all do. They share a spicy meal of burritos and tacos. Drink soft drinks and walk home through the midnight-blue park. They play cards until nine-thirty, when they say goodnight and curl up into their own pillowy beds. Hearts full of sobriety.

The next morning, they swim at the beach. Share another meal at a cafe. Bask in the sunshine with take-away coffees. Soon it is time to pack up and start the slow haul back to the clinic so James can finish his last few weeks of therapy. In the intimate space of the car for the one-hour drive between the rehabilitation clinic and the coast, Pearl, Elle, and James are looking for solace, understanding. James craves proof of their unwavering support. The fact they are here once more, after all he has done, is a testament to the profound love and closeness they share. Together, on this journey, Pearl, Elle, and James create a soundtrack of love, resilience, and unwavering familial devotion that will forever echo in their hearts.

* * *

It is late 2023. Elle is nearly forty and she reflects on her life's moments of chaos, calm, drama, romance, and horror. She has suffered trauma, overcome the peak of her anxiety, and escaped the clutches of toxic relationships. Moving into a life of simplicity and order with her kind-hearted lover, Bryce, and deep affection for their little boy, Elle feels an overwhelming sense of contentment. But the intergenerational trauma will take epochs to heal. The cyclical nature of addiction creates ripples throughout lives.

Elle's little life has been shaped by the criminal choices of her brother, Lance; James's life has been crippled by the insidious actions of his brother, Lance. Elle reflects, over a gin and tonic, how James's journey of recovery has been both helped and hindered by the ADF, DVA, and the pharmaceutical industry. The double-edged sword of support and enabling has influenced the outcomes of James's life and the web of lives connected to him, starting with Elle and Pearl. She sips her drink and rocks in the armchair on the deck. The light is fading and she can hear the television from the house next door quoting mundane facts. Asher is asleep and Bryce is in the kitchen, cleaning up after dinner. Elle feels a warm ray of gratitude wash across her body, hoping this feeling will last.

Everyone has a part to play in the recovery of a person with PTSD. Unfortunately, not everyone's part can be beneficial or positive. Sitting there, in the insect-singing dusk, Elle decides the only way she can heal properly is to write James's story. She sets about arranging her memories and tells Bryce of her plans. Over the next year, Elle will type and cry and laugh and weep some more. And the memoir of her dear brother James unravels and becomes her story and the shared story of familial abuse. As Elle writes, she heals and desperately hopes she can help heal others, starting with her brother James.

CHAPTER 39

James—Healing—2025

Knowing he will always be an addict is James's first real step towards recovery. All of the anger, the shame, the remorse, and the pain can sift through his fingers like grains of sand when he accepts the fact that he will always, *always* be an addict. The weight of his trauma is heavy, and at times it feels as though it will crush him whole. Other times, when he is feeling strong and astute, James uses his wicked sense of humour to laugh away moments of feeling uncomfortable and threatened. After so many years in therapy and the experience of rehabilitation, his toolbox is filled with coping skills. James is not silly—he can retain information and knows what he needs to do to stay sober. It's having the power, courage, and endurance to say no to the insidious clutches of addiction that is the biggest struggle.

He is at the end of his second long-stay rehabilitation treatment centre. It is a leafy clinic run by a private agency and James has survived three months of treatment and support. He is anxious about leaving, moving into another halfway house, and starting the road on recovery alone—again.

During one of his group therapy sessions earlier in the programme, James spoke about the downward spiral that led him back to rehab. Nervously twisting his fingers, he reminisced about how well he was feeling while living in the Northern Rivers, surfing every day, chasing waterfalls, and riding his motorbike. He could still feel the wind through his hair and smell the exhaust fumes as he buzzed along the highway. There was a clear-mindedness in sobriety—a clarity that made his body tingle. It was different to the numbing tingling sensation of using drugs. While the uppers made him energetic and feel invincible, once his chemical levels corrected through months of sobriety, he started to feel again. Like, *really* feel. The pain of the past was still there, but it had softened and James was able to keep his head above the waves of memories. With sadness, he longed to feel that way again: when the calmness within was tempered by his ability to stay sober.

Watching the group members' faces, some nodding with understanding, James admitted that life started to change after he received the compensation payout from the DVA. Eyes glimmered empathetically. Meeting Lily—oh, how he cared for her—James thought his life was perfect and he was healed. Now, in the honesty of the group, he reflected on the past three years and feels the old shame returning.

"One drink was too many and a hundred drinks was never enough." James shook his head in frustration. But it wasn't just because of the money, and it wasn't just because he met Lily, and it wasn't just because they travelled to Vietnam, and it wasn't any of these excuses he'd told himself over the past two years of using again. James knew that now. The addiction is loud, gnarly, and incessant. It would always give him an excuse to have another drink, search for a smoke of a pipe, or swallow more pills—although rehab had now taught him the skills and tools to silence the growling voice, ways to show gratitude for the wins, therapy to change the patterns he'd used to survive the PTSD.

Returning from Vietnam during the pandemic, Lily broke up with him once and for all, and James had nothing positive remaining in his life. He was used to having an abundance of oxytocin swimming in his brain while he loved Lily, while they laughed and travelled and made out. But when her side of the bed was empty, her toothbrush no longer in the bathroom, James was hollow. The emptiness led to boredom, which led to more drinking. Bottles and bottles filled his house, thousands of dollars pissed down the toilet. He could not wake up without a shot of vodka to ease the shakes. Soon, he was no longer making his own dopamine, so James increased the pharmaceuticals and overloaded his body with artificial chemicals, riding the highs and falling lower each come down. Burying himself under a toxic veil of poison. When the artificial dopamine wasn't enough to make him feel anything, James went back to Dr Wilson. She recognised immediately that he had been self-medicating and she suggested something that might or might not have been right.

"Remember when we first met, James?" Her gentle tone was reassuring.

He nodded.

"You told me about wanting to walk the Appalachian Trail." She leant back in her chair and crossed her legs. Watched James closely.

James was focusing on his sneakers, tapping his foot and trying desperately not to scratch at the scabs on his face.

"Yeah, I remember."

"You see, walking is very meditative, and it could be a good step on your road to recovery."

"Very punny." James smirked. It wasn't the time for being a smart-arse, but his mind began drifting back to the thoughts of freedom, wide open spaces, and starry, sober nights.

He left Dr Wilson's office with signed prescriptions for another three months' supply of medications.

James finished his story in the group session by saying thanks for listening. From there, he managed to recognise the triggers that led him back to using. Walking the Appalachian Trail had seemed like a good idea, yet he did not have a support network around him. Being alone in the wilderness only increased his anxiety.

Maybe, he thinks. *Maybe one day I will try it again. And not fuck it all up.*

* * *

Today, leaving the clinic after three months of treatment, with his army-issued duffel bag hoisted on his broad shoulders, James waits in the car park. Dragging deeply on his vape, kicking at a stone on the ground, he hears the low hum of an engine rolling along the crest of the hill. His phone pings. He pulls it from his pocket and sees a notification on the email app. Clicking on the shiny red icon, the email opens. James reads. He clicks his fingers and reads some more. When he is finished, he takes another inhale from his vape and tilts his head backwards. From deep inside the pit of his anxious stomach, James allows a wide smile to break through and he sends it high, high into the canopy of leaves, past the cerulean sky and beyond the powdery clouds. He hears himself chuckle alongside the rev of an engine. A white car turns the corner, coming into view and he is still grinning, ecstatic. It's his mum's car. Elle is waving from the passenger seat. Parking the car in the dappled light of the forest, the pair climb out of the car.

"Hi, brother," Elle says, beaming.

"Hey, sister."

The embrace is long, warm, and familiar. James pulls away and squeezes Elle's shoulders. Pearl swoops in for an even longer, tighter hug. Finally, she lets him go, wiping at her cheeks. James notices the deepened wrinkles on his mother's face.

They amble into the vehicle, Pearl and Elle up front and James stretching out along the back seat. Pearl pulls on the steering wheel and drives slowly along the curling road, snaking away from the rehabilitation clinic car park for what she hopes will be the very last time. Pearl asks James a few mundane questions that he answers politely. He is preoccupied with the spreading excitement through his cells, his limbs, his fingertips.

James reads the email once again. Next, he taps on the app icon for his bank account. Holds his breath as it loads and opens.

The numbers glide across the display in a series of six figures. Another compensation payout. Another opportunity to live the life he deserves.

James smiles. Speaks.

"Let's go. I'm never coming back here."

He glances up to meet Elle's eyes in the rear-view mirror and then, quickly, back to the screen of his phone. For a moment, James considers telling his sister and his mum about the money. But it doesn't feel like the right moment, not after what happened last time. And anyway, he is clean now, and he doesn't want to cause them any more stress. James closes his eyes and begins to imagine all the ways he will spend the money.